The SEN series

Surviving and Succeeding in Special Educational Needs

Fintan J. O'Regan MA (Management)

continuum
LONDON • NEW YORK

8424465

Continuum International Publishing Group

The Tower Building   15 East 26th Street
11 York Road   New York
London SE1 7NX   NY 10010

www.continuumbooks.com

© Fintan J. O'Regan 2005

British Library Cataloguing-in-Publication Data
A catalogue record for this book is available from the British Library.

ISBN 0-8264-7612-0 (paperback)

Typeset by Kenneth Burnley, Wirral, Cheshire
Printed and bound in Great Britain by MPG Books Ltd, Bodmin, Cornwall

Contents

Contents

Appendices

Introduction

This book provides information on the most common special education needs (SEN) for teachers and teaching assistants who are working within the inclusive school environment.

The main body of the book comprises 15 key SEN terms. Each entry includes facts on the main characteristics of the condition, ideas for managing students and useful resources, including contacts, websites and relevant publications. I am most grateful to the Hesley Group and OAASIS for allowing me the use of their materials in this section.

The rest of the book considers a variety of ways in which teachers can help SEN students, including a SEN directory of relevant support groups and additional information on the less common SEN. I am especially grateful to Pat Porter, the Special Educational Needs Coordinator of Salaesian College, London, for his assistance in compiling these details

Given the size of this publication, it has not been possible to concentrate in detail on the complete spectrum of SEN. However, I have done my best to provide an accurate and accessible introduction for everyone who wants to survive and succeed in SEN.

Part One

The World of
Special Educational Needs

The World of Special Educational Needs

The *Times Educational Supplement* reported in June 2004 that about one in four pupils in England and Wales is identified as having some form of special need. The number registered as having special needs has almost doubled, from 792,000 in 1995 to more than 1.5 million today. The degree to which students are affected ranges from mild to severe, but one thing is certain – around £3.6 billion is spent on special needs as a whole every year. More than two-thirds of this is spent on children with Statements.

There is no absolute definition for SEN. The Special Educational Needs and Disability Act (SENDA) of 2001 says a child has SEN if he or she has a learning difficulty which calls for special educational provision to be made for them. 'A child' includes any person under the age of 19 who is a registered pupil at a school. 'Needs' are judged not according to a predetermined scale of disability or achievement but in relation to how a child is doing in comparison to his or her peers. This is an open-ended definition that has generated ceaseless debate among educationalists.

The SEN 'Code of Practice' (2001) currently considers four main strands of special educational needs:

- Communication and interaction.
- Cognition and learning.
- Behaviour, emotional and social development.
- Sensory and/or physical.

Also, although medical conditions are mentioned, it is often the case that a specific medical condition does not imply that a child will have SEN. However, it will sometimes be the case that the medical condition affects the child's cognitive, behavioural, emotional and even physical state.

In addition, as stated in the 'Code of Practice', each child is unique, and often the many different learning styles are frequently interrelated. As a result, some children will have needs and requirements that fall into at least two or more areas.

There are a number of main categories of special needs which can be listed under the following headings.

Specific Learning Difficulty (SpLD)

This term describes a range of related conditions which occur across a continuum of severity. Pupils may have difficulties in reading, writing, spelling, or manipulating numbers, which are not typical of their genuine level of performance. Pupils may have problems with short-term memory, organizational skills, hand–eye coordination and orientation and directional awareness. Dyslexia, dyscalculia and dyspraxia fall under this heading

Emotional, Behavioural and Social Difficulties (EBSD)

This covers a continuum of severity and the full range of ability. It describes pupils whose difficulties present a barrier to learning and persist despite an effective school behaviour policy and curriculum.

At the milder end of the continuum, pupils have difficulties with social interaction and find it difficult to work in a group or cope in unstructured time. They may have poor concentration, temper outbursts and be verbally and/or physically aggressive to peers. Some pupils display signs of low self-esteem, under-achievement and inappropriate social interaction, but do not have behavioural outbursts and will be withdrawn, quiet and difficult to communicate with.

Other pupils provoke peers and are confrontational or openly defiant and sometimes physically aggressive towards adults. They have a short attention span. Their self-esteem is low and they find it hard or impossible to accept praise or take responsibility for their behaviour.

Some pupils cannot function in groups at all and exhibit persistent and frequent violent behaviour, which requires physical restraint.

As this term covers such a wide range of issues, and problems with behaviour are so closely associated with learning difficulties, it is necessary to look at some specific labels to describe the range of difficulties outlined above.

Attention Deficit Hyperactivity Disorder (ADHD)

This term is given to students who exhibit difficulties in concentration, impulsivity and who are often hyperactive. Three main forms exist:

* *Predominantly Inattentive Type (PIT)*. These are the students who appear to be mentally hyperactive on many occasions and who can in addition be impulsive. The ratio of boys to girls in this group is 1:1.
* *Hyperactive Impulsive Type (HIT)*. These are the students who can be most obvious by their actions. They

may appear 'driven by a motor' and are often students whose actions can lead them into severe academic and socialization problems. Boys appear in the ratio to girls of 4:1.

• *Combined Type (CT)*. This is when certain students exhibit criteria from both PIT and HT forms. (Full list of criteria in Appendix 2, pp. 114–15.)

Conduct Disorder (CD)

This is a category of behaviour difficulty where pupils often bully and show aggression to others. They may destroy property, including their own. (For a full list of diagnostic criteria, see Appendix 3, pp. 116–17.) If the condition occurs before age 10, then the prognosis for effective treatment is poorer than if the condition occurs after this age. The difference between students with CD and ADHD, for example, is often one of wilful intent. A student with CD is more likely to plan a specific situation, carry out the actions and may well develop an alibi for the situation. In contrast, the first time a student with ADHD thinks about what he has done is when he has already carried out the action.

Oppositional Defiant Disorder (ODD)

This is diagnosed when children display a certain pattern of behaviours that includes losing their tempers frequently, defying adults, being easily annoyed and deliberately annoying others (see Appendix 4, p. 118). It is a less extreme behaviour than Conduct Disorder, but left untreated it can overlap into associated areas such as Emotional, Behavioural and Social Difficulties (EBSD).

Tips on managing students with behavioural difficulties

- Minimize unnecessary movement around the classroom and use highly structured tasks with a clear aim and outcome to avoid off-task behaviour and disruption of others.
- Try to create a positive atmosphere.
- Consider body language and language used in communication.
- Consider position of resources – have all equipment on a table or given out to each child at the start of the lesson.
- Consider furniture arrangement – booths, rows or tables – so the teacher can see, give eye contact and reach the pupils easily and be mobile.
- Consider your position (eye-contact, physical proximity).
- Utilize the peer group – careful selection of where they sit, who they sit next to/opposite/near.
- Be flexible with seating arrangements – sitting alone, special place such as a booth or teacher's desk, not next to window or other distractions, re-arrange tables (possibly with space for time out) to suit the activity.
- Have clear routes round the room – consider who/what they pass.
- Agree rights, responsibilities and clearly defined rules/routines/classroom code (expressed positively) at the beginning of a term/year etc., discuss lining up, silent reading, listening when teacher speaks, etc.
- Make expectations clear.
- Set clear boundaries.
- Give explicit/specific instructions.

- Use the school reward systems and lots of positive rein-forcement; stamps, stickers, stars and good marks can be used for positive behaviours.
- Be consistent with approach and expectations.
- Give praise and encouragement often.
- Consider home/school liaison (a phone call is *very* effective and often quicker than referral).
- Try to avoid confrontation.
- Ignore inappropriate attention-seeking behaviour (if safe to do so).
- Set small, achievable targets each lesson.
- Reinforce appropriate behaviour by praising quiet/responsive children.
- Provide children with opportunities for responsibility and sense of belonging to the class, for example taking turns to give out equipment, reading, etc.
- Encourage positive self-esteem!

Autistic Spectrum Disorder (ASD)

Autistic Spectrum Disorder is a relatively new term used to denote the fact that there are a number of sub-groups within the spectrum of autism. All pupils with ASD share a triad of impairments in their ability to:

- understand and use non-verbal and verbal communication;
- understand social behaviour, which affects their ability to interact with children and adults;
- think and behave in a flexible manner – instead they often engage in restricted, obsessional or repetitive activities.

Some pupils with ASD have a different perspective of sounds, sights, smells, taste and touch, which affects their response to these sensations. They may have unusual sleep and behaviour patterns. In addition, they may have difficulty in understanding the communication of others and in developing effective communication themselves. Many are delayed in learning to speak and some may never develop speech.

Pupils have difficulty in understanding the social behaviour of others and in behaving in socially appropriate ways. They are literal thinkers and fail to understand the social context.

Pupils with ASD often do not play with toys in a conventional way but instead spin or flap objects or watch moving parts of machinery for long periods with intense concentration. They find it hard to generalize skills and have difficulty in adapting to new situations and often prefer routine.

Pupils with Asperger Syndrome are included in this category. Asperger pupils share the same triad of impairments but have higher abilities and better language development than the majority of pupils with autism.

Speech, Language and Communication Needs (SLCN)

Pupils with speech, language and communication needs have difficulty in understanding and/or making others understand information conveyed through language. The acquisition of speech and/or oral language is noticeably behind their peers and their speech may be unintelligible. Pupils with speech disorders have difficulties in producing speech sounds or problems with pitch or voice quality. They may stutter and have difficulties in using some speech sounds.

Pupils with language disorders find it hard to understand and/or use words in context. They may use words wrongly with inappropriate grammatical patterns and have a reduced vocabulary or find it hard to express ideas.

Tips for helping those with speech and language difficulties

- Gesticulate more than usual when addressing the child.
- Be aware of time management – give more input, without pressure to speak; give time to talk individually with child.
- Encourage group activities and language interaction.
- Use rhymes, finger-play, simple songs, singing games in small groups – joining in actions first without expectation of speech, particularly in French or Spanish.
- Give clear situations which require a response.
- Create multiple choices which require tick-box answers.
- Teach key words and make the child learn them.
- Use visual aids, models, pictures, diagrams, illustrations, demonstration, etc. so that they can understand lessons without language.
- Use mime to support spoken language.
- Leave out words for them to fill in with or without vocabulary box.
- Play naming games/labelling exercises.
- When pupils begin gaining fluency, use lots of oral work to practise, e.g. using everyday items to practise prepositions – 'The bag is on the chair', 'The bag is under the table', 'The book is in the bag'.
- Use lots of repetition with slight changes or use of same vocabulary in as many different situations as possible.

- Use lots of structured oral work in lessons.
- Use a bi-lingual dictionary so *you* can look up key words.
- Remember, when told off or asked to 'explain himself', such a boy may simply shrug his shoulders or look away, not out of disrespect but because he can't understand.
- Simulation, i.e. visual/perceptual.

Moderate Learning Difficulty (MLD)

Used to describe developmental delay across a number of areas. Pupils will have developmental delay across most subjects and have difficulty in acquiring basic literacy and numeracy skills and may have speech and language difficulties associated with intellectual delay. A few may also have low self-esteem, poor concentration, under-developed social skills and have behavioural, emotional and social difficulty and/or physical difficulty that affects their learning abilities.

Severe Learning Difficulty (SLD)

Used to describe students who have significant global delay and may also have mobility and coordination, sensory and communication difficulties and challenging behaviour. These pupils may have difficulty accessing the curriculum and may find it difficult to develop social skills.

Profound and Multiple Learning Difficulty (PMLD)

Used to describe pupils with more than one significant disability, which may include severe physical difficulties and a greater degree of intellectual impairment. They may require a high level of one-to-one support both for their learning needs and their personal care.

Hearing Impairment (HI)

A significant proportion of pupils have some degree of earing impairment. For educational purposes these pupils are regarded as having HI if they require adaptations to their environment through hearing aids in order to access the curriculum.

Hearing loss can be measured on a decibel scale and four categories are generally used: slight, moderate, severe and profound. Some pupils with a severe or profound loss communicate through signs.

A pupil who has experience of hearing and using speech may be able to speak but a child with a similar loss from birth would find verbal communication more difficult.

Tips for helping students with hearing impairments

- Make sure the room is bright enough to see visual cues or posters.
- Maintain normal speech but speak clearly for lip-reading.
- Do not talk when your back is to the child.
- Use gestures and facial expressions to aid understanding.
- Allow child to manage hearing aid in noisy situations.
- Stay close to the child during PE or in external situations.
- Seek guidance of the hearing impaired service and speech and language therapist.

- Seat proactively.
- Learn basic sign language.
- Teach other ways of communicating with the child.
- Use Teletext subtitles when watching TV.

Visual Impairment (VI)

This refers to a range of difficulties, from minor impairment through to blindness.

For educational purposes these pupils are regarded as having VI if they require vision adaptations to their environment and/or physical support through the provision of aids to access the curriculum. Pupils whose vision is corrected by spectacles should not be included in this group.

A blind pupil is usually defined as one who requires non-sighted methods for learning (for example Braille) and the use of their hearing. Other pupils with VI include those who are partially sighted or who have a restricted field of vision. They may use enlarged print or a mix of learning methods.

Tips for helping students with visual impairments

- Use a sloping desk.
- Use enlarged print in all materials.
- Use specialized software such as text HELP with a voice accompanying text on screen.
- Seat proactively.
- Allow more verbal explanations of work production: use of tape recorder, dictaphone.
- Explore the use of coloured paper, magnifying glasses, etc.
- Ensure that the classroom is well lit.

- Provide child with own books rather than sharing.
- Encourage independence.
- Use peer mentoring.
- Use brightly coloured balls and other equipment during PE.
- Teach word processing.
- Learn some basic Braille techniques.

Multi-sensory Impairment (MSI)

Many pupils with multi-sensory impairment, sometimes referred to as deaf blind, also have profound and multiple learning difficulties. They should only be included in this group if their sensory impairment is their greatest need.

The combination of deafness and blindness profoundly affects the pupil's perception of the environment and can result in high anxiety and multi-sensory deprivation. Pupils with MSI have to learn to communicate differently from those who are deaf or blind. Their other senses are used to supplement residual hearing and residual vision.

Physical Difficulty (PD)

Some pupils with physical difficulties are mobile, some walk without aids, and others may be wheelchair users. A few may be totally dependent on adults and unable to function independently. Pupils with PD may also have sensory impairments, neurological problems and learning difficulties.

There is a large number of conditions associated with PD which can impact on mobility; these include cerebral palsy, heart disease, spina bifida and hydrocephalus.

Some pupils with physical or medical problems have no problem in accessing the curriculum and learning effectively. In such cases, having a medical diagnosis does not imply that the pupil has SEN. In other cases, the impact on a pupil's education ranges from mild to severe. Pupils may need support in terms of physical access to buildings and classrooms to enable them to work properly.

Able, Gifted and Talented (AGT)

Though this is technically not listed as a special educational need in the 'Code of Practice', children who are able, gifted and talented have special needs. AGT is a term often associated with high intelligence but often a low threshold of attention/concentration skills which can result in a poor performance and/or a negative attitude to school work. The key element is that a special need should also include academic, athletic, artistic and social 'potential' being addressed in much the same ways as academic and social limitations will be (see Appendix 5, pp. 119–20).

Part Two

Key Terms in
Special Educational Needs

Asperger Syndrome (AS)

This is a disorder on the autism spectrum that causes restrictions to normal functioning in communication, socialization and imagination (in the ability to behave and think with any level of flexibility) and, often, in physical coordination. It affects boys and girls, but affects boys in significantly higher numbers.

Like many autism spectrum disorders, AS is a very individual syndrome. There will be wide variations in the physical and mental symptoms, in the degree of difficulties it presents, and in any early signs that parents noted. The presence of other disorders (see below) may confuse the issue.

Asperger Syndrome is known to coexist with other syndromes, such as Attention Deficit Hyperactive Disorder (ADHD), dyspraxia, Obsessive–Compulsive Disorder, speech and language problems, anxieties and phobias. People with AS are often nervous and anxious of any change in their lives and can become depressed about their lack of a social life, their inability to function independently at school or college, if they feel rejected by potential friends or employers.

Characteristics

* People with AS are sometimes described as having mild autism, but this is misleading and can undervalue the

significance of the diagnosis. There is nothing mild about the impact of AS. The effects are considerable and permeate almost every aspect of life.

- Sufferers may sometimes be described as having high functioning autism, but the two are usually diagnosed as separate conditions.
- People with AS are usually of average or above-average intelligence, and have good verbal skills.
- Usually, no significant language delay is noted during the early years.
- Good verbal skills mask a tendency to rely on literal meaning and an inability to read body language and facial expressions.
- Poor physical and visual–motor skills and clumsiness are seen as characteristics of AS. There are cases where these difficulties are not present.
- People with AS usually have a narrow range of interests, an adherence to specific rituals, and a pronounced lack of flexibility.
- Sufferers do not like change; they like 'sameness'. They are comfortable in their routines.
- People with AS make better efforts to adapt socially than do those with autism. They have a genuine desire to make social contact.
- Anxiety features significantly in the lives of those affected. Often the anxiety is related to low self-esteem, fear of failure, fear of being misunderstood and of not understanding others. There is also the anxiety associated with an awareness of being different and not fitting in.
- People with AS can be very egoistical and chauvinistic, and create impossibly high standards for themselves in all that they do.

Problems

Typically, a child with AS may encounter difficulties in primary school. The child is also likely to be exhibiting some disruptive behaviours – either at home, or at school, or both. This behaviour may have been odd and noticed at home from an earlier age, but may have been discounted by professionals as not being significant. If the child is the first in the family, the parents too may have thought that any slightly odd behaviours were either normal, or 'just him'.

Sometimes the transfer to secondary school takes place before real problems surface. The difficulties may not be academic (he is frequently top of the class). They are more likely to be because he does not understand the behaviour and intentions of those around him, the meanings of the instructions and lessons, or be able to interpret the wide variety of verbal and non-verbal language used by teachers and peers. The implications of AS are widespread in the social setting of the home or school.

Useful contacts

Autism Independent UK
Tel.: 01536 523274.

Care Training
Provides training around the UK for teachers, carers, parents.
Tel.: 01424 439691.

Contact a Family
Provides support and advice to families.
Tel. Helpline: 0808 808 3555.

The Hesley Group
Residential special schools for young people with special needs. Three of the schools and one Post-16 college take young people with Asperger Syndrome.
Website: www.hesleygroup.co.uk

The National Autistic Society
Can help with local support groups, information on Asperger Syndrome, advice, events and links.
Tel. Helpline: 0845 070 4004.

Resources for Autism
Affiliated to the NAS.
Tel.: 0208 458 3259.

Literature

A First Guide to Asperger Syndrome in the OAASIS *First Guide* series. £6 plus p&p. OAASIS (On-Line Asperger Syndrome Information and Support), Brock House, Grigg Lane, Brockenhurst, Hampshire SO42 8RE.
Website: www.oaasis.co.uk

Websites

www.asperger-syndrome.com   A site written by Ben, a 25-year-old man in London. Very good articles, including one written for younger children.
www.autism.org/contents.html   Home of the *Center for the Study of Autism*; many links, including information about siblings.

www.faaas.org   A site for families of adults with AS.

www.tonyattwood.com   Dr Tony Attwood's pages are a
mine of good information and articles.

www.udel.edu/bkirby/asperger   A very informative and
full American site, run by OAASIS. It covers autism as
well as AS, and has many papers and links to other AS
sites, some specifically for teachers.

www.users.dircon.co.uk/~cns   For university students
with autism and AS.

Attachment Disorder (AD)

Children who fail to develop secure attachments to protective and loving parents or other caregivers during their early infancy (0–3 years) may develop Attachment Disorder.

An infant whose primary requirements for food, water, love, comfort and security are poorly met or ignored will be anxious that future needs are not satisfied and become mistrustful. The anxieties that surround her own essential life-preserving needs gradually force the child to focus exclusively and aggressively on herself: her acquired insecurities, feelings of rejection and not being loved only kept at bay by being in total control of everything around her.

The behaviours associated with this may include aggression, both physical and verbal, against people and property; these young people may be oppositional, refusing to do as requested, no matter what the request. They will manipulate situations. In their teens they may seek consolation in alcohol, drugs or precocious, promiscuous sex. They may not see the truth as others see it. They will not respond to reason or logic.

Children with Attachment Disorder may have been bereaved, neglected or physically abused since very early infancy. It has been shown that children who did not succeed in making secure attachments as an infant may themselves become parents who are unable to offer their own children the material comforts of food and warmth, and the love and security which are essential to a healthy, happy, caring childhood. Instead, they in turn may abuse, neglect or abandon their own children.

Children with Attachment Disorder may:

* be superficially engaging, charming (phoney);
* avoid eye contact;
* be indiscriminately affectionate with strangers;
* lack the ability to give or receive affection;
* exhibit extreme control problems (e.g. stealing from family, secret solvent abuse, etc.);
* be destructive to self and others;
* lack kindness to animals;
* display erratic behaviour, tell lies;
* have no impulse controls;
* lack cause-and-effect thinking;
* lack a conscience;
* have abnormal eating patterns;
* show poor peer relationships;
* ask persistent nonsense questions and chatter incessantly;
* be inappropriately demanding and clingy;
* have abnormal speech patterns;
* display passive aggression (provoking anger in others);
* be unable to trust others;
* show signs of depression;
* exhibit pseudo-maturity;
* have low self-esteem;
* show signs of a guilt complex;
* show signs of repressed anger;
* sabotage placements such as school, foster family, etc.

Not all of these will be exhibited!

A young person with attachment problems needs to:

+ be able to respond positively to a significant other person;
+ comply to the basic rules of society;
+ comply to reasonable requests;
+ have a realistic sense of self;
+ learn to be non-confrontational with others;
+ accept responsibility for own actions;
+ feel valued;
+ fit into and accept the family dynamics;
+ manage temper/anger appropriately;
+ understand the world around him;
+ understand his own wants, needs and feelings;
+ have a sense of his own identity.

Meeting the needs

+ Provide a positive role model.
+ Create win/win situations.
+ Give clear, consistent guidelines and boundaries; allow some flexibility.
+ Be honest and truthful, with sensitivity to the young person's feelings.
+ Give calm, measured responses in confrontational situations.
+ Always endeavour to let them know it is *their behaviour* that is not liked, not them.
+ Tell them what behaviours annoy/irritate, and tell them why.
+ Allow your emotions to be seen: parents/carers are people too.

- Confront feelings in an open, honest way and help to build positive relationships.
- *Listen* to them: hear what they have to say. But remember, they communicate in more ways than just verbally.
- Plan *with* them for their adult life; help them to understand the attachment process and how they can be positive as an adult.
- Remember that the *adult* is responsible for helping young people make appropriate, positive attachments.
- Give the young person a safe, secure environment in which to express his innermost feelings, fears, hurt, etc.

Useful contacts

Adoption UK
Provides support, information and training for parents, foster carers, practitioners, teachers, etc.
Manor Farm, Appletree Road, Chipping Warden, Banbury, OX17 1LH.
Tel.: 01295 660121; fax: 01295 660123.
Website: www.adoptionuk.org.uk

The Children's Society
Works with young people of all ages, many of whom are without or separated from their families.
Edward Rudolf House, Margery Street, London WC1X 0JL.
Tel.: 0845 300 1128.
Website: www.the-childrens-society.org.uk

Family Futures Consortium
An assessment centre for families and children with attachment disorder.

35 Britannia Row, Islington, London N1 8QH.
Tel.: 0207 7354 4161.
Website: www.familyfutures.co.uk

Hurstwood Court

A small independent agency, providing a specialized service for children and families including assessment, therapies, residential care and education and a family placement service.
New Hall Hey Road, Rawtenstall, Rossendale, Lancashire BB4 6HR.
Website: www.keys-attachment-centre.co.uk

NCH Action for Children

The NCH has many regional offices. Addresses and phone numbers are on their website.
85 Highbury Park, London N5 1UD.
Tel.: 0845 7626 579.
Website: www.nch.org.uk

Post Adoption Centre

Provides independent advice, counselling and support to anyone affected by adoption.
5 Torriano Mews, Torriano Avenue, London NW5 2RZ.
Tel.: 0207 284 0555.
Website: www.postadoptioncentre.org.uk

WATCh (What About The Children)

A national charity promoting responsible, informed parenting and publicizing the emotional needs of children during their crucial first three years.
4 Upton Quarry, Langton Green, Kent TN3 0HA.

Tel.: 01892 863245.
Website: www.jbaassoc.demon.co.uk/watch

Literature

Archer, C. (1999) *First Steps in Parenting the Child Who Hurts – Tiddlers and Toddlers*. Jessica Kingsley Publishers.

Archer, C. (1999) *Next Steps in Parenting the Child Who Hurts – Tykes and Teens*. Jessica Kingsley Publishers.

Karen, R. *Becoming Attached*. Oxford University Press.

Websites

www.attach-bond.com
www.attachmentdisorder.net

Attention Deficit Hyperactivity Disorder (ADHD)

This is a medical diagnosis which has been used by the American Psychiatric Association since the 1980s to describe a syndrome of emotional and behavioural difficulties exhibiting core features of extreme levels of impulsivity, inattentiveness and motor activity.

Hyperkinetic Syndrome is the term used by the World Health Organization (the European guidelines) when comparing extreme levels of motor activity in children with 'normal' peers. It is now recognized as a sub-category of ADHD that applies to highly hyperactive children.

Three sub-types have been recognized:

◆ ADHD with hyperactivity (the 'hyperactive impulsive' type).
◆ ADHD without hyperactivity (predominantly 'inattentive' type).
◆ ADHD – Combined Type (see Appendix 2 for the full listed criteria, pp. 114–15).

It is estimated that in the USA between five per cent and seven per cent of children may suffer from ADHD. Because in the UK standards are organized in a different way, experts believe the rate to be between one per cent and five per cent. The condition is more common in boys, who are also more likely to be hyperactive.

Treatment

Most experts favour a multi-modal approach towards treating and managing the disorder, recognizing the coexisting conditions and the importance of treating all symptoms. Usually, the most effective form of therapy is in conjunction with other treatments.

At school, teachers need to help create a structured environment so that these children have fewer problems with starting and completing tasks, making transitions, working with others, following directions, organizing multi-faceted projects and maintaining attention. They need predictability, structure, short work periods, more individual instruction, positive reinforcement and an interesting curriculum.

Teachers should:

♦ appreciate and accept that children with ADHD cannot help themselves: their behaviour is not prompted by naughtiness;
♦ have positive expectations;
♦ monitor progress regularly throughout the lesson;
♦ give directions clearly and frequently and, wherever possible, visually (i.e. timetable);
♦ be consistent, firm, fair and patient;
♦ give constant feedback;
♦ display 'classroom rules' which are unambiguous and written in a positive way;
♦ make clear lists – these children need reminders which they can access themselves;
♦ repeat directions: write them, say them out loud more than once. Check that they understand;
♦ make lots of eye contact;

31

- make sure they know the boundaries: avoid long discussions about what is right and wrong in their behaviour: tell them what you want – give them the positives;
- avoid timed tests; these will not tell you what they know;
- do not set lengthy homework tasks: go for quality;
- break down each task into its smaller component parts;
- allow 'time out' if required;
- make learning *fun* – all children hate being bored.

At home, the child will need:

- structure;
- consistency;
- clearly defined boundaries;
- love;
- patience.

Drugs should only be prescribed by a doctor or consultant and they should be taken only as and when directed. Each individual reacts uniquely to medication: if one causes unwanted side-effects (such as weight loss, headaches or insomnia) then consult the GP again: the amount given, the time it is given, or the drug itself may need changing. There are several well-known drug treatments for addressing the problems posed to young people with ADHD. They can help increase attention, and reduce impulsivity and hyperactivity. Side-effects can occur in some cases.

Useful contacts

ADDISS (Attention **D**eficit **D**isorder **I**nformation and **S**upport **S**ervice)
For parents, sufferers and professionals. Keeps an extremely good book list and provides conferences and training.
Tel.: 0208 906 9068.
Website: www.addiss.co.uk; email: info@addiss.co.uk

The ADHD National Alliance
A group aiming to coordinate, promote and develop new work and work already being done across the country by various local ADHD support groups. It is supported by the Contact a Family charity. Membership is open to parents, professionals and support groups.
209–211 City Road, London EC1V 1JN.
Tel.: via Contact a Family: 020 7608 8760.

DC Educational Services
A charity which offers diagnostic testing (fee payable), counselling services, training and educational programmes.
6 Lower Grosvenor Place, Victoria, London SW1W 0EN.
Tel.: 0207 834 0033.
Website: www.dcedservices.com

Hyperactive Children's Support Group
Helps children, their families, teachers etc. and runs work-shops. Lots of information on foods and substances that affect children and teenagers with ADHD/hyperactivity.
71 Whyke Lane, Chichester, West Sussex PO19 7PD.
Tel.: 01243 551313.
Website: www.hacsg.org.uk

Literature

Breggin, P. R. (2002) *The Ritalin Fact Book: What Your Doctor Won't Tell You.* Available from Amazon (www.amazon.co.uk).

Cooper, P. and Ideus, K. (1996) *Attention Deficit/Hyperactity Disorder: A Practical Guide for Teachers* (ISBN 1-85346-431-7). David Fulton Publishers.

Cooper, P. and O'Regan. F. (2001) *Educating Children with ADHD* (ISBN 0-415-21387-8). Routledge Falmer (Tel.: 01264 343071; website: www.routledgefalmer.com).

Munden, A. and Arcelus, J. (2003) *The ADHD Handbook: A Guide for Parents and Professionals* (ISBN 1-85302-756-1). Jessica Kingsley Publishers.

O'Regan, F. (2002) *How to Teach and Manage Children with ADHD* (ISBN 1-85503-43488). LDA, a division of McGraw-Hill (Tel.: 01945 463441; email: ldaorders@compuserve.com).

Websites

www.adders.org   Thanet ADDers, where there is a list of local ADHD support groups run by parents.

www.mk-adhd.org.uk   ADHD Family Support Group, Milton Keynes, has superb information, tips, events, links etc.; useful wherever you are.

Autism

Children with autism exhibit, to a greater or lesser degree, a triad of impairment, which is the defining characteristic of autism:

* *Communication*: Language impairment across all modes of communication – speech, intonation, gesture, facial expression and other body language. People with autism have difficulty understanding the meaning of words, the intention of the speaker and are not able to interpret gestures, intonation, facial expressions or body language.
* *Imagination*: Rigidity and inflexibility of thought process: resistance to change, obsessional and ritualistic behaviour. People with autism have difficulty manipulating thoughts in an imaginative way. They may become unduly upset by any changes in their known pattern of life or routine. They may have a tendency towards repetitive actions within a restrictive range, such as body-rocking, hand- or arm-flapping.
* *Socialization*: Difficulties with social relationships, poor social timing, lack of social empathy, rejection of normal body contact, inappropriate eye contact. People with autism have little or no understanding of normal social interaction. They do not automatically make relationships and have difficulty understanding that other people have feelings, thoughts and intentions.

What causes autism?

To date, there is no clear answer to this question. It is believed to be present from birth in most cases, though there is debate about whether it can develop later. It appears to have some genetic predisposing factors and is associated with some types of brain damage. Work is being done on the possibility that allergies and dietary intolerances play a part. It is now clear that it is not caused by bad parenting – an idea which, thankfully, has been discredited.

It is unlikely that any single cause is going to be found. It is probable that a number of factors are operating together to give rise to the condition. As yet, there is no proven cure. As work progresses in this area it may be that prevention or improved treatment are a possibility.

What can teachers do to help?

Children with autism find listening and giving attention to the spoken word very difficult. Make it easier for them by keeping unnecessary 'chat' to a minimum, speak clearly and calmly, ensure you have their attention before speaking and allow lots of time for them to make sense of what you have said.

Also, be aware that children with autism may be extra-sensitive to sounds, light, touch, tastes and smells. They may dislike 'scratchy' materials next to their skin (i.e. wool) and may find sudden loud noises or bright lights very upsetting. Their daily environment should be autism-friendly – secure so that they cannot wander into unsafe areas, visually helpful as to what is in or behind cupboards, drawers, doors, etc. As well as being hypersensitive to some stimuli, children with autism may have very high pain thresholds, so any playtime or classroom 'accident' should be carefully checked.

To really make a difference to the education and care of individuals it is important to focus on the qualities and the strengths that an autistic spectrum disorder can bring. These qualities are many, and to maximise these can go some considerable way to improving self-esteem and confidence and alleviating many of the problems that the conditions represent.

Making a list of these qualities is a good place to start when looking to offer help. You could allocate a special role to a child of something they do well, either individually or in paired or small group work at school, or at home.

Professionals and families seeking to make a start on strategies to assist could also begin with considering the following general aims:

- Accept and respect individuals for their qualities, not in spite of them.
- Prioritize positive relationships. Be dependable and predictable yourself. Establish trust, and foster a sense of safety for them to be with you.
- Accept the diagnosis and the likely implications – even if you cannot readily 'see' the manifestation of it in the way you expected, or as instantly or as obviously as you expected. Individuals with ASD can be great at camouflage.
- Tailor learning to the specific needs of a child rather than make the child fit a process.
- Identify and offer safe places and safe strategies to facilitate expressions of anger safely.

- Reduce anxiety through predictability, routine, structure and warnings of changes.
- Adopt a non-confrontational approach to discipline and always take time to explain why behaviour is inappropriate – individuals may simply not understand or appreciate possible consequences.
- Increase relaxation opportunities/strategies and opportunities for space away from others.
- Consider the possibility of mood disorders, attention deficit or depression and whether extra support is needed.
- Increase independence and choice-making opportunities. (It can be helpful to limit choices.)
- Identify and reduce threats to self-esteem, confidence and safety.
- Consider what cues the individual responds well to and increase the use of them.
- Consider what rewards and treats are responded well to and increase their use.
- Acknowledge how over-sensitive individuals with ASD can be and avoid the use of harsh criticism, sarcasm and ambiguity that may cause confusion or embarrassment.
- Assess the immediate environment and its effect on any sensory issues that may be prevailing – over-acute sensitivity to light, noise, texture, smell, etc.
- Consider the issue of loneliness and isolation, and facilitate interactions with peers and contact with other young people experiencing similar challenges in life, either through local groups or the many Internet and email/pen-pal opportunities. Supervise any Internet access and seek safe sites.

Useful contacts

Autism Independent UK
199–205 Blandford Ave, Kettering, Northants NN16 9AT.
Tel.: 01536 523274.
Website: www.autismuk.com
email: autism@rmplc.co.uk

Contact a Family
Provides support and advice to families.
Tel. Helpline: 0808 808 3555.

The Hesley Group
Residential special schools and colleges for young people
with special needs. The schools cater for different groups,
e.g. autism/Asperger Syndrome; Asperger Syndrome/High
Functioning Autism; complex difficulties as a result of autism.
Website: www.hesleygroup.co.uk

The National Autistic Society
This organization can help with local support groups, publi-
cations and advice; they run their own schools and have a
diagnostic centre.
Tel. Helpline: 0845 070 400.
Website: www.nas.org.uk

Resources for Autism
Affiliated to the NAS.
Tel.: 0208 458 3259.

Literature

A First Guide to Autism in the OAASIS *First Guide* series.
OAASIS (On-Line Asperger Syndrome Information and
Support), Brock House, Grigg Lane, Brockenhurst,
Hampshire SO42 8RE. Website: www.oaasis.co.uk
Do You Know Someone with Autism? is a little booklet for
brothers, sisters and classmates of younger children
with autism. Available from OAASIS.

New books on autism autistic spectrum disorders are
coming out all the time. Contact the following:

David Fulton Publishers (tel.: 0500 618052; website:
www.fultonpublishers.co.uk; email:
orders@fultonpublishers.co.uk).
Jessica Kingsley Publishers (tel.: 0207 833 2307;
website: www.jkp.com; email: post@jkp.com).
Lucky Duck Publishing Ltd (tel.: 0117 973 2881; fax: 0117
973 1707; website: www.luckyduck.co.uk;
email: publishing@luckyduck.co.uk).
The NAS (HO Publications Dept, tel.: 0207 903 3595;
website: www.nas.org.uk). NAS books should be
ordered through Barnardos Despatch Services (tel.:
01268 522872; fax: 01268 284804; email:
beverley.bennett@barnardos.org.uk).

Websites

www.asperger.org   The site of ASC-US Inc. (formerly ASPEN), an American organization for people with autistic spectrum disorders.

www.autism-awareness.org.uk   A site run by the Disabilities Trust. It has news, events, a message board and publications.

www.autismmedical.com   The site for Allergy Induced Autism.

www.autism.org/contents.html   The *Center for the Study of Autism* site. Many links and sites for siblings.

www.autism-smile.co.uk   A home-based therapeutic play approach that enhances communication skills, language development and imaginative play and helps children interact more effectively.

www.autismuk.com   The website of Autism Independent UK; clearly laid out with much information.

www.autisticsociety.org   A site for parents, families and professionals, with a wide range of information, news, education, law, therapies, statistics, personal stories and much more.

www.mugsy.org   The website of the NAS (Surrey Branch). This is an excellent site with lots of up-to-date information, news, resources for wherever you are in the country.

www.udel.edu/bkirby/asperger   This is a very informative and full American site, run by OAASIS. It covers autism as well as AS.

www.users.dircon.co.uk/~cns   A site for students with autism and AS.

Cerebral Palsy (CP)

Initially called Little's Disease, after the English surgeon William Little who first wrote about it in the mid-nineteenth century, cerebral palsy is a blanket term for a number of disorders which affect muscles and movement.

If that part of the brain which controls movement is injured or fails to develop properly, a child may be born with or develop CP. At present there appears to be no single cause for CP, but medical research indicates that damage to the developing foetus from a viral infection, certain drugs, poor nutrition or prematurity may be a strong factor. To a lesser degree, low birthweight, lack of oxygen or injury during or just after birth, or cerebral bleed may also be attributable. It is thought that approximately two people per thousand of the population in the UK have CP.

Spastic CP

This is the most common form of CP. The person will have very stiff muscles and a decreased range of movements, making the most basic of activities extremely hard work.

If it affects just one half of the body it is described as *hemiplegic*. If both legs are affected (but not the arms) it is *diplegic*. If both legs and arms are affected, it is *quadri-plegic*.

Athetoid CP

The person will have frequent involuntary muscle movements, difficulties in controlling the tongue, diaphragm (breathing) and vocal cords, and hearing problems may also be present. Because of these problems, their speech may be difficult to understand until you get to know them well. This type of CP by itself is quite rare.

Ataxia CP

This affects the whole body: the person will probably be able to walk, but their balance will be affected and they will be generally uncoordinated. They will have jerky hand movements and speech.

Many people with CP will have a combination of the three types. As with many neurodevelopmental disorders, CP can affect people in widely different degrees of severity: no two people will be the same. But as always, try to see the person, not the condition.

Physical and mental characteristics

A child who has CP may have or develop some – not all – of the following, to some degree:

- limited movements;
- uncontrolled movements;
- muscle weakness;
- muscle stiffness;
- muscle spasm or muscle floppiness;

- speech problems;
- hearing difficulties;
- chewing/swallowing difficulties;
- squinting;
- epilepsy.

Treatment

A child born with cerebral palsy will always have the condition. It is not an illness, it is not contagious, it does not get worse, but on the other hand neither does it diminish with age. There are treatments and therapies which will help alleviate some of the symptoms of CP, and much can be done to help children manage their lives better. This includes your patience, understanding and willingness to look beyond the disorder – your efforts to do so will be well rewarded.

As always with a neurological disorder, a multi-disciplinary approach is advised. Children may need help from a range of professionals, including physiotherapists, occupational and speech and language therapists, and educational psychologists. Some children will need walkers, wheelchairs or protective headwear; some will need specially adapted knives, forks, spoons and writing equipment. For those whose speech is very difficult to understand, it will be easier for them to use a communication aid, whether this is a set of simple cards with words/pictures, or a sophisticated electronic speaking device.

Teachers should be aware that learning difficulties *may* be present, but this is not the rule: many children with CP have average intelligence and some may have above-average intelligence. If there are learning difficulties present, these may range – as in any population – from mild

44

through moderate to specific or severe. Perceptual or spatial difficulties are not uncommon, but are not always picked up.

Useful contacts

The Bobath Centre for Children with Cerebral Palsy
Offers neuro-developmental treatment for children and adults with CP and acquired neurological conditions.
Bradbury House, 250 East End Road, East Finchley, London N2 8AU.
Tel.: 0208 444 3355.
Website: www.bobath.org.uk

Capability Scotland
ASCS, 11 Ellersly Road, Edinburgh EH12 6HY.
Tel.: 0131 313 5510; Textphone: 0131 346 2529.
Website:www.capability-scotland.org.uk

Cedar Foundation
Formerly the Northern Ireland Council for Orthopaedic Development.
1 Upper Lisburn Road, Belfast BT10 0GW.
Tel.: 028 9062 3382; website: www.cedar-foundation.org

The Foundation for Conductive Education
A registered charity for children and adults with motor disorders. It strongly challenges present ways of understanding and providing for disabilities.
Cannon Hill House, Russell Road, Moseley, Birmingham B13 8RD.
Tel.: 0121 449 1569.
Website: www.conductive-education.org.uk

SCOPE

Largest registered charity working with adults and children with cerebral palsy.

The Helpline offers free information, advice, initial counselling and parent training.

Runs own schools and college, residential and small group homes, community teams.

CP Helpline, PO Box 833, Milton Keynes, MK12 5NY.
Tel.: 0808 800 3333.
Website: www.scope.org.uk

Scottish Centre for Children with Motor Impairments

A centre and school for children with CP, based on conductive education and the Scottish Curriculum. There is a medical adviser and a family support worker.

1 Craighalbert Way, Cumbernauld, Glasgow G68 0LS.
Tel.: 01236 456100; fax: 01236 736889.
Website: www.craighalbert.co.uk

Websites

As well as the above, see the following for helpful information and articles:

www.healthsystem.virginia.edu/pediatrics   Children's Medical Centre of the University of Virginia (click on 'Tutorials').

www.ninds.nih.gov/health_and_medical/pubs/cerebral_palsyhtr.htm   The USA's National Institute of Neurological Disorders and Stroke.

www.abilities.fsnet.co.uk   A website set up by Gillian Archbold, a parent, and Sabrina her daughter with CP. They offer support, advice, information booklets and training. Has a fun section for children to access.

Down's Syndrome

A baby will have Down's Syndrome if it is born with an extra whole or part of chromosome 21, giving her 47 chromosomes instead of the usual 46. It is a genetic condition, and for the majority of people with Down's Syndrome there is no specific reason why the mutation has occurred: it is not the result of anything the parents did or did not do. The extra chromosome can come from either the father's sperm or the mother's egg cells, or can occur just after conception. Women who conceive after they are 35 appear to be particularly susceptible to having a child with Down's, but the age of the father does not appear to have a similar effect. If a couple has one child with the syndrome, then their chances of having another are increased. Genetic counselling is advised. There are pre-natal tests which will be offered to prospective parents by their GP or health centre if there is any reason for concern. The most common test (at present) is the amniocentesis test, when a sample of the amniotic fluid, which surrounds the foetus in the woman's uterus, is assessed.

The syndrome is named after Dr John Langdon Down who first described it in 1866. At present there is no treatment or cure for the condition, but advances in genetic manipulation may eventually provide answers.

Down's Syndrome occurs in around one out of every thousand births, in both girls and boys. It can affect anyone, regardless of race or background. It is said to be the most common cause of learning difficulties.

Characteristics

A child who has Down's Syndrome will be affected in both growth and development, but each child is an individual and will be different. Not all children with Down's will display all of the symptoms, and some children who appear to have the physical characteristics will *not* have Down's Syndrome. Although the child with Down's Syndrome will share some physical features with others who have the disorder, like any child she may also look like her mother, her father and her brothers and sisters. The child with Down's will have some moderate learning difficulties.

Some of the physical features of Down's Syndrome include:

* low birth weight and length;
* slanting eyes;
* flat bridge to the nose, giving the face a rather flat appearance;
* rather flat back to the head;
* low, somewhat uneven hairline at the neck;
* small mouth, but large tongue, causing it to protrude a little – training can minimize this;
* reduced muscle tone, which improves with age;
* smaller-than-average height.

Other conditions which someone with Down's Syndrome may also have:

* heart problems;
* hearing problems;
* thyroid disease later in life;

* weight problems;
* dry skin;
* coughs and colds.

Developmental milestones will be reached on average some months or years later than is considered the norm. The children are generally very happy, fit and healthy. Some years ago people with Down's Syndrome often did not survive much past young adulthood, but many now live well into their 50s and beyond, and early thought and planning will ensure that their adult lives are as satisfying as possible.

Management hints

* A multi-disciplinary approach is advised and should include advice and intervention from, for example, physiotherapists and occupational, speech and language therapists.
* A controlled diet and exercise plan should be provided. Children with Down's do not grow as tall as other children, and they can easily put on weight. A doctor and health visitor will be able to supply diet sheets, growth charts, etc.
* Most will need a Statement of Special Educational Needs so that any extra resources they require can be provided.
* In their teen years, an independent living skills programme should be an important component of their formal education to let them move on, when they are ready, to some form of sheltered living.

Teachers should be aware that, because of low muscle tone and developmental delays, Down's Syndrome children will take longer than others to learn ordinary childhood skills such as running, jumping, skipping, throw-and-catch, doing up buttons, laces and buckles, and handwriting. They will also need regular hearing and sight tests.

Always check that the child has understood what is expected of her by asking her to repeat what she has to do. Make sure she can see and hear you clearly. Inform your classroom teaching assistant of her problems; check regularly with the parents – they are your experts, and will know if their child is enjoying, or dreading, coming to school.

Both parents and teachers should encourage, praise, build confidence and self-esteem at all times: an ultimate goal of everyone should be a child who is as happy, independent, self-reliant and self-motivated as possible. She will probably know that she is different; our concerns should be to reduce the negative impact of this for her, while acknowledging that we are *all* different, and to make sure that she can enjoy the same rights and privileges as everybody else.

Useful contacts

Down's Syndrome Association
Langdon Down Centre, 2a Langdon Park, Teddington TW11 9PS.
Tel.: 0845 230 0372; fax: 0845 230 0372.
Website: www.dsa-uk.com;
email: info@downs-syndrome.org.uk

The Scottish Down's Syndrome Association,
158/160 Balgreen Road, Edinburgh EH11 3AU.
Tel.: 0131 313 4225; fax: 0131 313 4285.
Website: www.dsscotland.org.uk;
email: info@dsscotland.org.uk

Both organizations offer advice and support to parents,
carers and professionals.

Websites

www.43green.freeserve.co.uk   A website run by Chris
    Gravell, a parent, which contains loads of information
    including extensive list of support groups.
www.cafamily.org.uk   The Contact a Family website has
    information and articles.
www.dsa-uk.com   This is the Down's Syndrome Associa-
    tion's website. It includes excellent information for
    teachers, as well as downloadable booklets for
    parents, grandparents and others.
The Scottish DSA is at www.dsscotland.org.uk

Dyslexia

Dyslexia is a specific learning disability, sometimes called 'word blindness'. Dyslexia is said to affect approximately one out of every ten pupils in the UK, from all walks of life, and with all levels of intellectual ability. It generally affects boys to a greater degree of severity than girls. It tends to run in families, and recently a gene has been identified which scientists believe may be responsible for dyslexia. For some 60 per cent of people with dyslexia, the sounds which go to make up words are also a problem and many children will find the skills required for basic maths difficult. However, many people with dyslexia have strong creative talents in the arts, design, computing and lateral thinking.

During a child's early school years, dyslexia may affect his self-esteem to such an extent that, until it is properly diagnosed and remedial teaching put in place, the child may refuse to read or write, appear 'stupid' to his peers, and generally find life very confusing and worrying.

The signs

Does the child have any of the following?

- A history of late speech development, and continuing immaturities in articulation and syntax.
- Visual perception problems – frequent reversal of letters and numerals, distorted or blurred word shapes.

- Auditory perceptual problems, including difficulties in identifying sounds within words and blending sounds into words.
- Poor integration of sensory information. For example, they cannot easily learn to associate and remember printed symbols and their spoken equivalent.
- Weak lateralization – under-developed hand–eye preferences, directional sense confusion.
- Hyperactivity.
- Weak sequencing skills, reflected in jumbled letter sequences in spelling or in word-attack skills in reading.
- Poor coordination.
- Low level of motivation.
- Secondary emotional problems due to learning failure and poor school progress.

Some hints for the classroom

- Reading, writing, spelling and maths skills should be thoroughly taught – leave nothing to chance.
- The skills must be utilized in a meaningful way so that reading, writing and arithmetic are used for a real purpose, not merely as drill exercises.
- Ideally, provide special tuition, perhaps by withdrawing the child from the regular class for brief, intensive, regular sessions. Where this is not possible, individual help should be given daily within the classroom setting.
- Read to him every day, as he follows the words with you.
- Provide daily opportunities to read and write for real purposes.
- Teach reading skills in context, rather than in isolation.

- Surround the child with stimulating reading material.
- Create a climate where reading is an enjoyable, relaxing, necessary and valued occupation.
- Give abundant encouragement and praise as the child masters new skills.
- Systematically teach phonic knowledge and word-building, unless contra-indicated by speech or auditory problems.
- Skills should stem from, and be applicable to, the actual reading material being used by the child.
- Teach correct letter formation and handwriting along-side the reading activities.
- Use finger-tracing and other multi-sensory approaches to aid assimilation and retention.
- Be careful to select material to match the child's current ability and interest level.
- Revise and review previously taught skills or concepts at frequent intervals.
- Practice and over-learning are vital for success.

Useful contacts

Artificial Relevance

Produced 'linstines', a computer-based dyslexia-screening programme. You can obtain a demo from Flat 3,
133 Torrington Park, London N12 9AN. Also 'read-e', which is a dyslexia-friendly web browser at www.read-e.com
Tel.: 07906 260258.
Website: www.artificialrelevance.com;
email: info@artificial-relevance.com

British Dyslexia Association

Information for parents, employers, teachers.
Their website talks and can change colour.
98 London Road, Reading, RG1 5AU.
Tel.: 0118 966 8271; fax: 0118 935 1927.
Website: www.bda-dyslexia.org.uk;
email: admin@bda-dyslexia.demon.co.uk

CReSTeD (Council for the Registration of Schools Teaching Dyslexic Pupils)
Holds a list of schools which have met certain criteria for dyslexia-friendly education.
Greygarth, Littleworth, Winchcombe, Cheltenham, Glos. GL54 5BT.
Tel./Fax: 01242 604852.
Website: www.crested.org.uk

Dyslexia Inspirations

Activities and downloadable information for parents and teachers, produced by teachers. Work packs to order.
PO Box 243, Swansea, SA3 1YA.
Tel: 01792 390625.
Website: www.dyslexia-inspirations.com

Dyslexia Institute

Educational charity for assessment and teaching of dyslexic people; training of specialist teachers.
Park House, Wick Road, Egham, Surrey TW20 0HH.
Tel.: 01784 222300.
Website: www.dyslexia-inst.org.uk;
email: info@dyslexia-inst.org.uk

Literature

Pumfrey, P. and Reason, R. (1991) *Specific Learning Difficulties (Dyslexia): Challenges and Responses*. London: Routledge.

Websites

www.brightstarlearning.com   A programme enabling dyslexics to reach their full potential.

www.dyslexia-net.co.uk   An Internet forum for students with dyslexia.

www.dyslexic.com   A website for information and products together with www.iANSYST.co.uk, a training centre.

www.literacytrust.org.uk and www.nla.org.uk

www.penfriend.biz   A CD for computers, helping people to write faster, more accurately and with less effort.

www.s-a-i-d.com   A site for parents.

www.tintavision.com   Enabling Access to Text with Asfedic tuning to discover the correct computer colours for individuals.

Dyspraxia

Also known as Developmental Coordination Disorder or Motor Learning Difficulties, dyspraxia refers to children who have movement difficulties. Approximately one in ten children suffer from the condition, with boys affected four times more frequently than girls. In a class of 30 children, at least one will have dyspraxia.

Teachers and parents may notice the problem early on: their child may have trouble with some of the following:

- dressing, e.g. doing up buttons, tying shoe laces;
- picking up small objects;
- left/right orientation;
- concept of in/on/behind, etc.;
- riding a bicycle, PE, ball games;
- drawing or copying a drawing;
- holding a pencil;
- doing a jigsaw or sorting game.

There might also be some speech and language or pronunciation difficulties caused by problems in coordinating the various movements of the mouth and tongue.

Help for home and at school
Dressing

- Use Velcro on shoes: not laces or buckles.

- Wear loose clothing.
- Avoid ties – they are very difficult.
- Shirt buttons: use larger holes and buttons.
- Socks: wear short ones if possible, as long nylon socks are difficult to handle.
- Wear clothes with a distinctive front and back; for example, a V-neck sweater.

Other support strategies for teachers and parents

- Give clear, simple instructions.
- Develop alternative mediums of output, i.e. use of ICT and tape recordings of information.
- Develop motor coordination activities.
- Use writing frames.
- Develop sequencing activities.

Social integration

Offer lots of public praise at the appropriate time, but ensure that other children in the class or group do not begin to feel that this is unfair treatment. Always pick good points from the child's work. Make certain that other children are praised for their efforts at the same time.

Give them some responsibilities/tasks which should involve others; encourage teamwork.

Encourage the child to 'join in' with other pupils, by helping them to find and develop common interests such as music, fashion, etc. Encourage other children to help the child to join in, to improve skills, and dissuade them from isolating him.

Insist that *all* the social rules of the classroom/

home are observed. Although this may seem painful at times, the child needs to be the same as his peers and observe the same rules. This helps the children to heighten their own awareness of behaviour.

Pupils with dyspraxia need considerable support from significant adults with regard to their social interactions. Depending on the degree of severity, they will also benefit from regular interventions from some of the following: educational psychologists, orthoptists, occupational therapists, physiotherapists and speech therapists.

Useful contacts

Anything Left Handed Ltd
All staff are left-handed; they produce a range of items and have a fact sheet on handwriting for left-handed children.
18 Avenue Road, Belmont, Surrey SM2 6JD.
Tel.: 020 8770 3722.
Website: www.anythingleft-handed.co.uk

British Dyslexia Association
98 London Road, Reading, RGH1 5AU.
Tel.: 0118 966 8271.

Dyscovery Centre
Assessment and advice on dyslexia and dyspraxia.
4a Church Road, Whitchurch, Cardiff CF14 2DZ.
Tel.: 029 2062 8222.
Website: www.dyscovery.co.uk

The Dyspraxia Foundation

Support and information for individuals, families and professionals affected by dyspraxia.
8 West Alley, Hitchin, Herts SG5 1EG.
Tel.: 01462 454986.
Website: www.dyspraxiafoundation.org.uk

Dyslexia Institute

Park House, Wick Road, Egham, Surrey TW20 0HH.
Tel.: 01784 222300.

The Foundation for Conductive Education

A registered charity for children and adults with motor disorders. It strongly challenges present ways of understanding and providing for disabilities.
Cannon Hill House, Russell Road, Moseley, Birmingham B13 8RD.
Tel.: 0121 449 1569.
Website: www.conductive-education.org.uk

Handwriting Interest Group

National body which aims to raise standards of handwriting in schools and support children with handwriting difficulties.
5 River Meadow, Hemingford Abbots, Huntingdon, Cambs PE28 9AY.
Website: www.handwritinginterestgroup.org.uk

Literature

Macintyre, C. (2000) *Dyspraxia in the Early Years: Identifying and Supporting Children with Movement Difficulties* (ISBN 1 85346 677 8). David Fulton Publishers.

Portwood, M. (1999) *Development Dyspraxia: Identification and Intervention – 2nd edition: A Manual for Parents and Professionals* (ISBN 1 85346 573 9). David Fulton Publishers.

Portwood, M. (2000) *Understanding Developmental Dyspraxia: A Textbook for Students and Professionals* (ISBN 1 85346 574 7). David Fulton Publishers.

Ripley, K., Daines, R. and Barrett, J. (1993) *Dyspraxia: A Guide for Teachers and Parents* (ISBN 1 85346 444 9). Includes resource materials. David Fulton Publishers.

Websites

http://homepage.ntlworld.com/dorothy.mcgregor/dyspraxia/index.htm   Set up by a parent, with lots of useful information, including a draft letter to request a visit by an educational psychologist.

http://matts.hideout.users.btopenworld.com   An excellent website set up and run by a 13-year-old boy who suffers from dyspraxia.

www.dyspraxiafoundation.org.uk   The Dyspraxia Foundation site.

www.unix.oit.umass.edu/~velleman/cas.html   A US paper on apraxia (verbal dyspraxia) with a link to www.apraxia.org (Childhood Apraxia of Speech Association).

Epilepsy

Epilepsy is not an illness or a disease: it is a tendency of the brain to produce a spasm, seizure or fit if something triggers it. Seizures or fits happen when the neurones in the brain suffer a temporary malfunction. For someone to have epilepsy, they must have experienced repeated seizures or fits over a period of time: a single episode does not warrant the term 'epilepsy'. There are an estimated 440,000 sufferers in the UK. Anyone can develop it, regardless of age, race or sex, but onset is usually before the age of 20 or after 65.

Causes

Sometimes there is no apparent reason for a seizure. In other cases, epilepsy may start in childhood or adolescence and be due to the brain's own idiosyncrasies rather than from brain damage due to a disease or injury. It may also be acquired as the result of some form of brain damage or as the result of another medical condition, for example a diffi-cult birth, a head injury, severe head infection, a stroke or a brain tumour. Photosensitive Epilepsy is relatively rare and only affects about three per cent of people with the condition. Photosensitive Epilepsy responds well to med-ication.

Diagnosis

There may be no external indications that someone has epilepsy, and a doctor can only begin to make a diagnosis if more than one seizure has occurred, by questioning the patient, and using, if at all possible, the observations of any witnesses to the seizures. Diagnosis may also require other tests, such as blood tests, brain scans and EEGs.

Treatment

Epilepsy can be controlled, sometimes completely, with appropriate drug treatment.

Self-help

People with epilepsy can reduce risks to keep their seizures to a minimum, by:

- making sure they get enough sleep;
- drinking alcohol moderately;
- avoiding emotional upsets;
- avoiding trigger stimuli such as strobe lights;
- taking all medication strictly as directed.

Seizures

There are two types of seizures: *generalized* or *partial*.

Generalised seizures

The whole of the brain is involved and consciousness is lost. Seizures may be major convulsions with limb-jerking and unconsciousness; the body going stiff or floppy, together with unconsciousness; or limb-jerking and momentary lapses of consciousness. Breathing may be noisy and irregular, and some people may suffer incontinence.

Partial seizures

Here the disturbance in brain activity starts in or involves one *part* of the brain. Seizures are very individual but the seizure type will depend on which area of the brain is involved. There are three types of partial seizure: simple, complex and secondary generalized. In simple partial seizures, consciousness is not impaired. The seizure may be confined to either rhythmical twitching of one limb, or unusual tastes or sensations such as pins and needles in parts of the body. In complex partial seizures, consciousness is affected and the person may have no memory of the seizure. The seizures may involve a change in awareness as well as automatic movements such as fiddling with clothes or objects, mumbling, chewing, or wandering about and general confusion. Secondary generalized seizures occur when a simple or complex partial seizure develops to encompass the whole brain. The result is a convulsive seizure, loss of consciousness and confusion afterwards.

Children and epilepsy

In the main, epilepsy should not cause problems either for the child or for his classmates and teacher. As with many problems, good communication between home and school is essential. Parents should not be worried to tell the school about their child's epilepsy, and teachers should be willing to listen and learn about the child's particular form of the condition. Detailed knowledge about the frequency and type of seizures, any triggers, etc. is necessary so that as normal a life at school as possible can be achieved.

What to do during a seizure

Seizures may look worrying, but the thing to remember is that the person having the seizure is not aware of what is happening, and is not in pain. Most seizures do not require medical intervention. At the start of an attack, it is not uncommon for breathing to stop temporarily and the person turn blue until breathing restarts. This is normal. Once started, you should not try to stop an attack, and remember:

- Reduce embarrassment to everyone: limit the number of people standing around; once any convulsions have ended and if the person has been incontinent, deal with it quietly, privately and matter-of-factly; be as reassuring and normal as possible afterwards.
- Do not try to stop the convulsive movements.
- Do not attempt to put anything in the person's mouth: they will not swallow their tongue.
- If possible, make them comfortable by putting something soft under their head.
- Do not try to move them unless they are in a dangerous place, such as a road.
- Once any convulsions have stopped, put the person into the recovery position.
- Check breathing and airways. If breathing is irregular or absent, check the mouth for obstacles.

- Make a note of the type and length of the seizure – the person or their family may wish to know.

Attacks which do not involve convulsions and loss of consciousness can vary tremendously: be prepared. You may need to stay with the person as a calm and sympathetic presence; if they wander around, you may need to help them keep clear of obvious dangers such as stairs. Confusion often follows such a seizure and may be present for some time. Allow the sufferer to recover in their own time without undue interference: they may react in an apparently unfriendly way if constantly spoken to.

When to call for medical help

- If the person has hurt themselves during the seizure.
- If they cannot breathe following an attack.
- If a seizure is followed quickly by one or more further seizures.
- If the seizure lasts for more than five minutes and the usual length of this person's seizures is unknown.
- If the seizure lasts for longer than you know is usual.

Sudden Unexpected Death in Epilepsy (SUDEP)

Cases of death apparently resulting from epilepsy rather than other factors are being researched. These are usually referred to as Sudden Unexpected Death in Epilepsy, or SUDEP. It is thought that there are around 500 cases a year in the UK when someone with epilepsy dies unexpectedly and for no apparent reason. Those most at risk seem to be 20–40-year-olds. Contact Epilepsy Bereaved, tel.: 01235 772850; website: www.sudep.org

Useful contacts

Epilepsy Action (formerly The British Epilepsy Association)
Everything you need to know about epilepsy for sufferers, including teenagers, parents and carers.
New Anstey House, Gate Way Drive, Yeadon, Leeds LS19 7XY.
Tel.: 0113 210 8800; free Helpline: 0808 800 5050.
Website: www.epilepsy.org.uk;
email: helpline@epilepsy.org.uk

Epilepsy Scotland
Useful material plus local support group information.
48 Govan Road, Glasgow G51 1JL.
Tel.: 0141 427 4911; free Helpline: 0808 800 2200.
Website: www.epilepsyscotland.org.uk;
email: enquiries@epilepsyscotland.org.uk

NCYPE (The National Centre for Young People with Epilepsy)
Run a national assessment centre, on-site resource centre, St Piers School up to age 16 and a further education college.
St Piers Lane, Lingfield, Surrey RH7 6PW.
Tel.: 01342 832243.
Website: www.ncype.org.uk

The National Society for Epilepsy
Information, support, respite care, rehabilitation and long-term residential care. They produce an award-winning information pack, covering all aspects of epilepsy and learning difficulties.

Chesham Lane, Chalfont St Peter, Bucks SL9 0R.
Tel.: 01494 601300; Helpline: 01494 601400.
Website: www.epilepsynse.org.uk

Literature

Contact the above for their reading lists, plus:

Appleton, R. (1995) *Illustrated Junior Encyclopaedia of Epilepsy* (ISBN 0 94827 060 8). Libra Pharma Ltd: Petroc Press. For children over 10.

Appleton, R., Chappel, B. and Beire, M. (1997) *Your Child's Epilepsy: A Parent's Guide* (ISBN 1 87236 261 3). Class Publishing.

Johnson, M. and Parkinson, G. (2002) *Epilepsy: A Practical Guide*. David Fulton Publishers. Resource materials for teachers.

Lears, L. (2002) *Becky the Brave* (ISBN 0 807560 601 X). Aiber and Whitman. A story for children about epilspesy.

Websites

www.epilepsyawareness.co.uk   Provide tailor-made training courses for a variety of authorities and organizations.

Fragile X

This is recognized as the most common form of inherited learning disability, caused by a gene defect in the X chromosome. The disorder may be passed on from one generation to the next. It can occur in both boys and girls, but is twice as common in boys, at an incidence of approximately one in 4,000. Learning disabilities vary considerably from mild to severe.

Diagnosis

Many cases of Fragile X go undetected: people may be unaware of its presence in their families and in themselves. This is because some people who carry the damaged gene might not be affected by it at all. They can, however, pass it on to their children. DNA testing can detect Fragile X in children and adults. In the unborn child, diagnosis can be by amniocentesis or by CVS (chorionic villus sampling) as early as ten weeks. This testing may not always distinguish affected from unaffected carrier females.

The genetics

The inheritance pattern in Fragile X is very complex, and it may be present for many generations before it causes any problems. Once a diagnosis has been made, parents should see a genetic counsellor to discuss the implications for their family. Very briefly, the FMR1 gene that causes Fragile X is on the X chromosome. A woman has two X chromosomes (XX); a man has one X and one Y chromosome (XY). It can be passed on by a woman or a man who has an affected X chromosome, to a child of either sex.

Characteristics

Boys are more severely affected than girls. This is possibly because girls have two X chromosomes, and the unaffected one may partly be able to compensate for the other.

Cognitive

The range of abilities is wide. A majority of boys with Fragile X will have some form of learning disability ranging from moderate to severe. Girls are usually less affected.

Physical

The physical features of Fragile X may be very subtle, and are seldom so marked as to give an unusual appearance. Some people with Fragile X may have heads that are larger than average, long faces, large jaws, protruding ears and high palates and dental overcrowding.

Behavioural

Behaviours can vary considerably. People with Fragile X can exhibit many autistic-like features, such as high anxiety in a crowded or noisy place, hand-flapping, spinning, and a dislike of direct eye contact. They are comfortable in routines they know well, and will find changes stressful. They like the company of others and do not avoid social contact, although their autistic-like reactions to some situations may give rise to misunderstanding. The main problems appear to be impulsivity, inattentiveness and, especially in boys, hyperactivity. They may have motor coordination problems. Speech and language difficulties are common: speech may be repetitive, with strong use of learned stereotypic phrases. They may have trouble staying on topic, will throw in inappropriate comments, impulsive replies, and will talk at varying speed and volume.

Treatment

There is no cure for Fragile X at present. Treatment should be multi-disciplinary, with input from the family's medical team, the child's school, speech therapists and occupational therapists. Medication may be suggested to improve concentration, and may be required if epilepsy is also present. Early intervention is highly recommended.

Hints

Many children with Fragile X will be seen initially as relatively able, as they have high verbal abilities and will be alert to what is happening around them. They also have a good sense of humour and are good imitators. Their visual skills are good and they will learn better if visual clues and aids are used: their auditory skills are generally weaker. Their reading and spelling abilities may be higher than their comprehension skills. Mathematical skills, however, are usually poor.

Teachers and parents should be aware of the 'overload' effects of too much sound, movement, touch and even smell and taste. The resulting anxieties may produce non-stop chatter, total withdrawal, or autistic traits such as hand-flapping or hand-biting. Their anxieties and coordination problems may limit their use of playthings such as swings, bicycles, etc.

In general

* Use the child's interests, ability to mimic and his sense of humour as much as possible.
* Use lots of visual clues to augment auditory instruction.
* Break tasks down into small units.
* Prepare the child well for any changes to established routines.
* Keep all distractions to a minimum.
* Do not talk excessively; allow time for instructions to be assimilated, or answers given.
* Do not give too many instructions at once.
* Reinforce and encourage all attempts at speech.
* Bring the level of your speech to that of the child. Allow the child to work in small groups and, because of their ability to mimic, preferably with higher-functioning children.
* Maintain close home/school contact so that goals can be synchronized.

Associated problems

Some people with Fragile X may also develop epilepsy, and there is a tendency to short- or long-sightedness, squints, and – in children – recurrent ear infections (glue ear).

Useful contacts

Fragile X Society
Rood End House, 6 Stortford Road, Great Dunmow,
Essex CM6 1DA.
Tel.: 01371 875100.
Website: www.fragilex.org.uk

Literature

Dew-Hughes, D. (ed.) (2003) *Educating Children with
    Fragile X: A Multi-Professional View*. Routledge Farmer.
Saunders, S. (1999) *Fragile X Syndrome – A Guide for
    Teachers*. David Fulton Publishers.
Weber, J. Dixon (2000) *Children with Fragile X Syndrome:
    A Parent's Guide*. Woodbine House.

Websites

www.fragilex.org.uk   The Fragile X Society.
www.cafamily.org.uk/Direct/f33.html   Contact a Family.
www.bdid.com/fragilex.htm   From the USA, a page of
    other links (including an email support group).

Obsessive–Compulsive Disorder (OCD)

This is a fairly common, treatable, neuropsychiatric disorder.

To have a diagnosis of OCD, someone must have excessive, intrusive and inappropriate obsessions (uninvited thoughts which occur over and over) and/or compulsions (repetitive, sometimes senseless actions which have to be performed physically or mentally). The person with OCD has no control over her obsessions and compulsions; they arrive without warning and without being initiated; they will not disappear just because she does not wish to entertain them.

It is not known exactly what causes OCD, but it *is* known that it is not the sufferer's fault or the result of a weak or dysfunctional personality or family background. Some research has suggested that genes may play a role in some cases, and it is known to run in families, particularly when it is first seen during early childhood. It is far more common than most people realize; in the USA approximately one in 50 adults currently has OCD, and numerous cases go unrecognized and unreported for many reasons. Not all obsessive–compulsive behaviours are unusual or disabling; some are welcome and supportive rituals, such as daily prayers, bedtime stories, kissing on parting, etc. Only when the rituals become persistent, senseless, cause anxieties and distress or make normal life impossible – for the sufferer or people close to her – do they need to be addressed.

Unlike psychotic disorders such as schizophrenia, people

with OCD usually know what is real and what is not, and that often their thoughts, or the actions they need to do, make no sense to others.

There is no instant cure for OCD, but its symptoms can be controlled by either drugs and/or cognitive behaviour therapy. Symptoms can be quite disabling on some occasions; less so on others.

Common obsessions can be fears of something happening to one's family or self, contamination with dirt/germs/toxins, symmetry or the 'evenness' of things, numbers, actions or bodily functions. Sometimes an obsession may be concerned with sexual/aggressive urges, religious or moral concepts or taboos.

Common compulsions often involve actions surrounding anxieties: some may be intricate and highly repetitive rituals to protect the individual or others from harm or to bring good luck and, once started, are unstoppable: 'What would happen if I didn't . . . ?' Many are repetitive or checking actions: saying something out loud or in one's head over and over; checking that windows/doors are locked before leaving the house. Others involve excessive hand-washing, cleaning, counting, hoarding or saving things, touching objects or people, doing everything precisely, perfectly and slowly, or obsessional praying. Some compulsions may be the avoidance of something (possibly that is associated with their obsession), or asking for reassurance all the time.

Problems

Time

The obsessions and compulsions of someone with OCD can take up an enormous part of their waking hours. If the

OCD sufferer is a child, the resulting behaviours and time involved with their rituals can become extremely frustrating for parents, friends and teachers.

Anxiety

Some obsessions and compulsions can cause the sufferer huge embarrassment, anxiety and, in extreme cases, depression. Unusual, sexual or aggressive obsessions or compulsions can be severely disabling because of the mental agonies that the person goes through each time a thought intrudes, or if he has to perform his compulsion.

Other disorders which may be seen with, or confused with, OCD

*   *Asperger Syndrome, autism.* Both have stereotypical behaviours which can be confused with OCD, but someone with OCD does not have the communication and social skills deficits of AS and autism.
*   *Body Dysmorphic Disorder* or 'imagined ugliness disorder' can be an OCD obsession.
*   *Depression* and OCD in adults is not uncommon, but people with OCD are not generally depressed or sad.
*   *Disruptive behaviours* may result from OCD.
*   *Learning disorders* such as ADD, ADHD, may be made worse by OCD.
*   *Phobias.* OCD is an acute anxiety disorder, and people *could* have more than one!
*   *Nail-biting and skin-picking* can be present in autism as well as OCD. These actions may respond to the treatments prescribed for OCD.

- *Stress* can exacerbate OCD symptoms.
- *Tourette's Syndrome* resembles OCD when it presents with touching or tapping tics.
- *Trichotillomania* (compulsive hair-pulling) may be part of the OCD range of activities, or a Tourette's tic.

Treatments

A doctor or consultant will discuss those current treatments which may be suitable and appropriate for the child. Behaviour therapy may be one option, medication another – or a mixture of both. Research evidence indicates that for children, the optimum treatment is a combination of both responses.

Behaviour therapy

This will probably start with an in-depth assessment of the obsessions and/or compulsions. This may mean the child and her family keeping a detailed diary of when problems arise. Strategies will be offered to help the child be in control of her problems one step at a time. It is important that the child is fully involved with detailing her own behaviour modification tactics, so that she feels fully comfortable with any programme that she will have to follow. Parents, other family members, and sometimes close friends, also need to know what is involved, so that they too can help.

Medication

This has been shown to help about 70 per cent of people with OCD. It provides more 'instant relief' than behaviour therapy, and that's why a combination of both is recommended for children with the disorder. The drugs used are the same as those prescribed for depression and other anxiety disorders. They are chosen because they act on the brain chemicals – specifically serotonin, which is the chemical responsible for the communication between different parts of the brain. All medicines should be taken exactly as prescribed, and any side-effects reported to the child's doctor. If you are not happy for the child to take drugs, or if the prescribed drugs are unsuitable, then behaviour therapy can be used alone.

Remember

- OCD is a disorder, not a personality trait; OCD is nobody's 'fault'.
- Be supportive, understanding, sympathetic – and patient.
- Encourage and support the sufferer and any treatment put in place.
- Do not encourage or support the obsessions and compulsions!
- As far as possible, do not let the obsessions or compulsions force you to adapt home or school life.

Useful contacts

First Steps to Freedom
Help with OCD/anxiety disorders/phobias.
1 Taylor Close, Kenilworth, Warwickshire CV8 2LW.
Tel.: 01926 864473.
Website: www.first-steps.org

National Phobics Society
Offers help with local support groups, advice/counselling, home visits.
Tel.: 0870 770 0456.
Website: www.phobics-society.org.uk

OCD Action
UK support group for sufferers and their families.
Tel.: 0207 226 4000.
Website: www.ocdaction.org.uk

Literature

Foster, C. H. (1994) *Polly's Magic Games: A Child's View of OCD.* Dilligaf Publishing.
de Silva, P. and Rachman, S. (1998) *OCD.* Oxford University Press.
Hyman, B. and Pedrick, C. (1999) *The OCD Workbook: Your Guide to Breaking Free from Obsessive–Compulsive Disorder.* New Harbringer Publications.
Marks, I. (2001) *Living with Fear.* McGraw-Hill.
Thomsen, Per Hove (1999) *From Thoughts to Obsessions: OCD in Children & Adolescents.* Jessica Kingsley Publishers.
Waltz, M. (2000) *OCD: Help for Children & Adolescents.* O'Reilly.

Websites

As well as any mentioned above:

www.ocfoundation.org   US-based site.
www.psychnet-uk.com/dsm_iv/obsessive_compulsive_disorder.htm   A UK-based site.
www.nomorepanic.co.uk   Clear, easy-to-use site with lots of information and advice.
www.triumphoverphobia.com   Information and details of a treatment programme.

Prader-Willi Syndrome (PWS)

This is a genetic disorder first identified by three Swiss doctors in 1956: Drs Prader, Labhart and Willi. Its features include food obsession, shortness of stature and poor muscle tone. It affects boys and girls alike, and occurs in families from all backgrounds. It is estimated that one in every 10,000 to 12,000 births will have the disorder. It is the most common known genetic cause of life-threatening obesity in children.

Research indicates that PWS may be the result of four different genetic abnormalities on chromosome 15. In approximately two-thirds of cases there is a *deletion* on chromosome 15 coming from the father. In about 30 per cent of cases, both copies of the chromosome are inherited from the mother, instead of one from her and one from the father. If you have one child with PWS it does not necessarily follow that you are any more likely than the population at large to have another, but genetic counselling is advised. Genetic testing is by DNA (blood) sample of both partners and the affected child.

Early indications

PWS, being a genetic disorder, is present from birth. In the very early months parents may notice that their baby has difficulty sucking, is very quiet and sleepy compared to other babies, and appears to be very 'floppy'. Later, from about six months to a year, their baby will become more alert and awake as the tendency to sleep recedes, but the early feeding problems will be replaced from the age of 2 onwards by an almost insatiable desire to eat, although the intensity of this feature will vary considerably between individuals.

Physical characteristics

These may include short height, very small hands and feet, narrow face, small mouth, almond-shaped eyes and under-developed sexual organs. It has also been noted that up to half of Caucasian children with PWS will be fair-haired and have blue or grey eyes, regardless of their parents' colouring.

Developmental delays

Motor and language skills will be affected, resulting in late walking and talking plus problems with articulation.

Behaviour

In their early years the children are friendly, loving and placid, but behavioural difficulties usually set in and become more severe as the children grow and they have to cope with their insatiable desire for food. Stealing and hiding food may become common activities as the obsession grows, and many outbursts of temper and rage can be put down to these 'needs' being necessarily moderated by their parents or carers. Others may relate to any change in their accepted daily routine which will upset them. Anxiety and worry may result in compulsive skin-picking and other similar self-injurious behaviours.

Other possible characteristics are a high pain threshold, sleep disorders, breathing difficulties, curvature of the spine and physical inactivity. Psychiatric problems are not uncommon in adolescents and adults.

In general

Comprehension is generally better than verbal skills. Moderate learning difficulties across the board are common, but severe learning difficulties are rare. Many individuals will have specific difficulties with maths, writing, short-term memory and auditory processing.

Children with PWS have good visual organization (parents have observed a higher than average ability to do jigsaw puzzles), good reading skills and a wider than average vocabulary. When they are older they may be over-friendly, chatter a lot, be immature compared with their peers and be socially isolated.

The majority of affected children will experience the syndrome into adulthood, and as long as their general health stays good and their tendency to obesity can be controlled, their life expectancy will be much the same as the general population.

Hints

* As with many disorders, a multi-disciplinary approach is advised and should include input from physiotherapists, occupational and speech and language therapists.
* GPs will often make a referral to a dietitian/nutritionist for a controlled diet and eating plan.
* Encourage a daily exercise routine from a very early age: seek help from local sports centres.

- It is not a good idea to use food as a reward with these children! Try a rewarding trip to the swimming pool, gym, walk on the beach or in the countryside.

Teachers should be aware that their student with PWS may have problems with:

- coordination;
- handwriting;
- maths;
- abstract concepts;
- attention span, especially if required to listen for 'long' periods;
- socializing skills;
- controlling their hunger;
- controlling their temper, particularly if they want to eat and food is withheld;
- worries and anxieties involving all the above which may result in minor self-injury.

Useful contacts

Gretton Homes

Gretton Homes is a group of eight residential holistically run care homes supporting 50 PWS clients.
Gretton House, 3 High Street, Gretton, Northants NN17 3DE.
Tel.: 01536 770325.

The Prader-Willi Syndrome Association (UK)

Offers support and advice to parents and professionals.
125a London Road, Derby DE1 2QQ.
Tel.: 01332 365676.
Website: www.pwsa-uk.demon.co.uk

Semantic Pragmatic Disorder (SPD)

This is a communication disorder. It is believed that people with SPD are unable to process all the given information from certain situations. The disorder relates in some way to autism because children with SPD have difficulties in the same three areas called 'The Triad': socializing, language and imagination.

SPD is often described as the 'outer spectrum of autism', but all children with features of autism will have semantic and pragmatic difficulties with language. It is always best therefore to have a specialist medical consultation to exclude autism or find out where your child might be within the ASD spectrum and if he or she has any additional problems with attention or dyslexia. Children with SPD may also behave very differently at home from at school, and parents' concerns should always be taken seriously.

At every moment we are automatically (subconsciously) absorbing information, processing and analyzing it, discarding what is irrelevant and storing what is important or salient. We use this to build up a bank or memory of words and meanings, like time and feeling words, which have no visual reference. When we speak to someone we use our past experiences to predict their moves, their intentions and their wants and we imagine what might happen next. People who have difficulties with this form of processing will have problems with understanding what is appropriate to say. They may appear too rude or outspoken, and not be aware when the other person has 'had enough' – SPD children will talk at length on topics like *Thomas the Tank Engine*, dinosaurs and *Star Trek*, and are often genuinely surprised when they find that not everyone is so enthusiastic! Children with SPD will cope with straightforward instructions ('Give me the red book'), but may have difficulties in responding to 'What have you been doing today?' as it is not explicit enough.

Children with SPD will relate best to sensitive adults but need a helping hand with peer relationships.

Characteristics

Children with a semantic pragmatic communication disorder may show some of the following features (but not all) in their early school years:

* Sound very grown-up.
* Be a fluent speaker, but on their terms.
* Have difficulties giving specific information on one event.
* Show no appropriate eye contact/facial expression exchange.
* Have problems with abstract concepts ('Next week . . .'; 'Guess . . .').
* Do not ask teacher for help.
* Do not ask children to play with them.
* Can appear rude, arrogant, gauche.
* Can embarrass others.
* Be a late reader or very early reader – but with little understanding.
* Be over-active *or* too passive.

- Follow rules, and expect others to.
- Be aloner, *or* over-friendly.
- Be bad at team events and games.
- Have a dislike of crowds.
- Have food fads.
- Be bad at social events (school breaks, parties).
- Show some motor skills problems (writing, drawing, bike riding, dressing, football).
- Be over-sensitive to some noises or tastes.
- Be easily distracted in a busy environment.

These children need:

- to learn from practical hands-on tasks;
- a quiet, orderly working environment – with visual clues;
- predictability to reduce their anxieties – i.e. turn-taking and changes in routine clearly signalled;
- small work-groups, good role models, special small communication group activities;
- simple instructions spoken slowly – do not bombard with questions or non-specific orders, e.g., say 'Put the toys in the box', not 'Tidy up';
- time to reply when asked a question, but replying *for* them – on occasions – can help understanding;
- help with socializing – specific games, role-play;
- clear rules on how to behave using concrete language they can understand;
- constant positive reminders supported by visual/written information;
- everything written down – i.e. clear timetable, instructions, message for mother;
- a diary between home and school – on a daily basis if

possible – with regular information on topic work to facilitate pre-tutoring and shared information;

* *constant* encouragement and praise.

Other tips

* Try to respond to his *intentions*, not what he actually
  says, as this may not make sense.
* Explain sarcasm, metaphors, jokes, when you use
  them.
* Employ 'mapping' technique (matching your words to
  the child's thoughts).
* Double-check he understands by asking him what is
  expected of him.
* Utilize his special 'interests' rather than ignoring or
  banning them.
* Make him feel useful by giving him regular little jobs,
  e.g. wiping board, putting out pens.
* Always allow him to observe other children first.
* Teach the meanings of useful idiomatic expressions and
  appropriate playground language.

Useful contacts

AFASIC
Advice, support, information, publications, activity holidays,
training.
2nd Floor, 50–52 Great Sutton Street, London EC1V 0DJ.
Tel. Helpline: 0845 355 5577.
Website: www.afasic.org.uk/

Communications Forum

A registered charity set up in 1994 to bring together the organizations concerned with the needs of people with speech and language impairments.

Camelford House, 87–89 Albert Embankment, London SE1 7TP.

Tel.: 0207 582 9200.

Website: www.communicationsforum.org.uk

I CAN

Advice, support, special schools, information for parents and professionals.

4 Dyers Building, Holborn, London EC1N 2QP.

Tel.: 0845 225 4071.

Website: www.ican.org.uk

NAS

Nationwide organization for people with autistic spectrum disorders.

393 City Road, London EC1V 1NE.

Tel.: 0207 833 2299.

Website: www.nas.org.uk

Royal College of Speech and Language Therapists

Contact them for availability of local speech therapy.

White Hart Yard, London, SE1 1NX.

Tel.: 0207 378 1200.

Website: www.rcslt.org

Websites

See Useful Contacts above, plus:

www.asperger.org   ASC-US Inc. (formerly ASPEN), an American organization for ASD.

www.mugsy.org   The Surrey NAS website is excellent for autistic spectrum disorders: use their search facility and you will find many good links.

www.talkingpoint.org.uk   A clear, informative website with separate sections for parents and professionals: covers many areas including information, support and education. Developed by I CAN, RCSLT and Afasic.

www.udel.edu/bkirby/asperger   An excellent site in the US on Asperger Syndrome which also has good links to other speech and language websites.

Tourette's Syndrome (TS)

This is a hereditary, neurological disorder characterized by motor (body) or vocal tics, which become apparent by the age of about 15. The tics are irresistible and their severity will come and go from one day to the next. Many people with TS do have some control over their tics, but the tics may well reappear with renewed vigour once the control is relinquished. Things often improve as the young person reaches adolescence. The tics can be very distressing for the young person, causing embarrassment and possible teasing from friends and even family. It is much more common in boys than in girls.

All children with Tourette's Syndrome will have tics of some sort. They are very difficult to control, and the process of trying to keep them to a minimum can be the cause of constant stress and anxiety. Try to keep this uppermost in your mind when dealing with TS.

Recently, this disorder has gained much wider recognition following a couple of excellent television programmes, and several well-known people have described how TS has affected them in their school, social and working lives.

Characteristics

The most common motor tics may include:

*   eye-blinking or eye-rolling;
*   squinting;

* nose-twitching;
* lip-smacking;
* tongue-thrusting;
* shoulder-shrugging;
* arm-extending . . . and others.

The most common vocal tics may include:

* throat-clearing;
* grunting;
* spitting;
* swearing;
* stammering;
* hissing;
* shouting, barking, moaning . . . and others.

Associated symptoms

Other symptoms can include moodiness, compulsions, obsessions and impulsions, echolalia/palallia (repeating of phrases/words or syllables), coprolalia/copropraxia (speaking/gesturing obscenities), stuttering, apraxia (non-neurological inability to carry out an action, such as reading).

Other syndromes often associated with Tourette's are Attention Deficit Hyperactivity Disorder, anxieties including phobias, Obsessive–Compulsive Disorder.

Problems

The young person with TS may be quick to lose her temper, may over-react in certain situations, will have difficulties with impulsivity, and may display defiant behaviour to those in authority. At school they may have problems organizing their work, playing/working quietly, speaking at the appropriate time (they may interrupt others, or encroach on their space, work area, etc.). They may appear not to listen to the teacher; they may lose vital papers, books, other items necessary for school or home activities. They may take part in physically hazardous activities without having thought through likely outcomes.

Treatment

Certain drugs such as clonidine or haliperidol can control TS and its associated tics. A doctor will advise you. Any medication given needs to be closely monitored so that it can be adjusted according to the progress of the disorder. Drugs often have some side-effects in some patients.

Hints for school and home

* Do not draw attention to the tics: try to ignore them.
* Allow 'time-out' periods for her to express her tics privately in a safe place. This will help avoid an outburst in the classroom or at home.
* In class, allow the pupil to sit near the door for an easy, non-disruptive exit when necessary.
* Ensure the pupil is not being teased or bullied by her peers, siblings or other relatives.
* Focus on the behaviour you *want* to reinforce: the more attention paid to the positive behaviour, the more likely she is to repeat it.
* Find a reward that is satisfying – concentrate on rewarding only one or two behaviours at a time.

+ The reward system chosen must be closely monitored and reviewed (over-use of rewards will lead to diminishing returns).
+ Ensure that medication is regularly monitored.
+ Avoid confrontational situations: aim to divert attention.
+ Be consistent when issuing sanctions. Negotiate these sanctions with the pupil beforehand in order that she understands the consequences of any aggressive or anti-social behaviours.
+ Be consistent with approaches in all aspects of the pupil's life. Do not allow the pupil to receive mixed messages from different people.
+ All agencies (parents, teaching staff, psychologists, etc.) must work closely together.

Useful contacts

The Tourette Syndrome (UK) Association
This organization has helpful leaflets and a reading list. There is also a 'Doctor On-line' section of their website where you can contact a doctor with any questions you may have.
PO Box 26149, Dunfermline, West Fife KY12 7YU.
Tel. Helpline: 0845 4 58 1252; Administration: 01383 629600.
Website: www.tsa.org.uk; email: enquiries@tsa.org.uk

Websites

The TSA(UK) site is at www.tsa.org.uk where you can order its information packs.
Two US-based sites: The Mental Health pages on TS are at www.mentalhealth.com/book/p40-gtor.html and the TSA Inc. site is at www.tsa-usa.org

Williams Syndrome (WS)

This is a rare genetic condition giving rise to both physical and mental disabilities. Research indicates that it is caused by a deficiency in the gene that controls the synthesis of elastin.

The condition can be difficult to ascertain without a blood test (known as the FISH Test) and often the disorder can remain undiagnosed for many years.

Characteristics

People with Williams Syndrome have characteristic facial features that become more pronounced as the child grows. They are not always noticeable on an individual basis, but when a group of WS people is observed together they do become more apparent. Sometimes only a trained geneticist will be able to see these traits.

Children with WS may:

+ be small for their age;
+ have low-pitched voices;
+ have super-sensitive hearing;
+ be excessively anxious or fearful;
+ have a short attention span;
+ display obsessive behaviours;
+ be hyperactive;
+ be overly friendly – show no shyness of strangers;

- have language delay;
- have poor communication skills.

Children with Williams Syndrome will tend to show overall developmental delay and learning difficulties, from mild to severe. Some display disproportionate abilities in some areas, however, and many have very good memories.

Social

They are loveable and sociable children, and empathize easily with others' feelings. They will chatter non-stop, and are eager to please, especially adults. It has been observed that although they are very outgoing and disinhibited with adults, their peer group relationships are not as good. They are nearly always excessively anxious children, fearful for the welfare of friends, family and strangers, of heights, imagined disasters and unknown situations. They may be inappropriately friendly with people they do not know, and 'stranger-danger' should be taught early. Appropriate greetings to various people should also be taught and practised regularly.

Language

Although their language may have been delayed in their very early years, by school age their verbal skills are often superior to those of other children in their year group. They will speak fluently and correctly, with an excellent vocabulary, but this may conceal some inadequacies of comprehension. They may have very little skill in taking turns in a conversation, and maintaining a subject appropriately.

Medical

Children with WS may suffer from heart problems, including murmurs, infantile hypercalcaemia (high levels of calcium in the blood or urine) resulting in feeding problems, irritability, constipation and sometimes kidney disorders. Children with WS may also have dental problems and raised blood pressure. They are often of small stature and build.

Motor skills

They will probably have coordination problems, and difficulties in the areas of visual–spatial information, in sequencing and construction tasks.

At school

Their poor attention and communication skills will require sympathetic and consistent interventions. They will work best in a quiet and distraction-free environment, and they are likely to need some one-to-one guidance from an adult in order to complete tasks successfully. Teachers should not ignore the usefulness of a reward system for doing as they are asked for a certain length of time, and consider making use of any specific interests the child has – if they liked watching the fish in the fish tank, or looking at a favourite book, make this their reward for sitting still during story time. However, many children with Williams Syndrome have good memories, and some may have specific talents, i.e. musical ability. Nurture these!

If their way of getting your attention or responding to their own frustrations is a temper tantrum, then firm and consistent handling is important. They must see that you will not give in to them, or pay them any attention, until they calm down. Do not confuse them by giving in one day, but not the next. If tantrums occur frequently, try to monitor what has led to the event: is it a sudden noise (school bell), a particular child or teacher coming too close, or even moving from one task to another. If you can discover a trigger, then it might be possible to either remove the trigger, or the child, just before the next occasion.

At home

Feeding, sleeping and toileting problems are associated with Williams Syndrome. Many young children have fads with the food they will accept. Some refuse all 'lumpy' textures or new tastes. New flavours and textures should be explored, however, as fussy eaters will cause problems at school. Reward them for trying one spoonful of a new food at a meal. If they have raised levels of calcium they may need to be put on a low-calcium and Vitamin-D-restricted diet. A GP/consultant will advise.

The sleeping problems may be part of their all-encompassing anxiety. A firm and consistent approach is needed, and establishing a relaxing, enjoyable and regular routine at bedtime will ease anxieties. Leaving a light on, a favourite toy, lullabies and reassuring words will all help.

Toileting is a difficult area, and you may find it best to ask a health visitor or local health clinic nurse for advice.

The young person with Williams Syndrome will find dressing and undressing difficult. Allow them extra time, and break down any long, complicated tasks into smaller components: teach one skill at a time. The following might help also:

- Use Velcro on shoes rather than laces/buckles.
- Wear clothes that are not too tight.
- Avoid ties – they are very difficult.
- Shirt buttons: larger holes and buttons.
- Socks: short ones if possible – long nylon socks are difficult to handle.

Useful contacts

For more information and to find out if there is a support group near you, contact:

The Williams Syndrome Foundation Ltd
161 High Street, Tonbridge, Kent TN9 1BX
Tel.: 01732 365152; fax: 01732 360178.
Website: www.williams-syndrome.org.uk

Literature

Contact the WSF above for their reading list.

Part Three

Directory of
Key SEN Organizations

Directory of
Key SEN Organizations

ADDISS (Attention **D**eficit **D**isorder **I**nformation and
Support **S**ervice)
For parents, sufferers and professionals. Keeps an
extremely good book list and provides conferences and
training.
Tel.: 0208 906 9068.
Website: www.addiss.co.uk; email: info@addiss.co.uk

ADD/ADHD Family Support Group UK
Site for parents and professionals related to ADHD.
1a High Street, Dilton Marsh, Westbury, Wiltshire
BA13 4DL.
Tel.: 01373 826045.
Website: www.addcontact.org.uk

ADDNET UK
National website for ADHD.
Tel.: 020 8260 1400 or 020 8516 1413.
Website: www.btinternet.com/~black.ice/addnet

Advisory Centre for Education (ACE)
Provides parents with advice on all aspects of education,
including SEN.
Unit 1C, Aberdeen Studios, 22 Highbury Grove, London
N5 2DQ.
Advice line: 0808 800 5793 (Monday–Friday 2–5pm).
Website: www.ace-ed.org.uk

Alliance for Inclusive Education (ALLFIE)

Supports inclusive education for all children.
Unit 2, 70 South Lambeth Road, London SW8 1RL.
Tel.: 020 7735 5277; website: www.allfie.org.uk

Association of Workers for Children with Emotional and Behavioural Difficulties

For those who work with children who have emotional and behavioural difficulties.
Charlton Court, East Sutton, Maidstone, Kent ME17 3DG.
Tel.: 01622 843104.
Website: www.awcebd.org.uk

British Association of Teachers of the Deaf (BATOD)

Organizes meetings and publishes a journal on education of hearing-impaired children.
21 The Haystacks, High Wycombe, Bucks HP13 6PY.
Tel.: 01494 464190.
Website: www.batod.org.uk

British Deaf Association (BDA)

Information and advice related to hearing impairment.
1–3 Worship Street, London EC2A 2AB.
Tel.: 020 7588 3520.
Website: www.britishdeafassociation.org.uk

British Dyslexics

Provides free information, advice, assessment and support to parents of children with dyslexia.
22 Deeside Enterprise Centre, Deeside, Chester CH5 1PP.
Info line: 01352 726656; Tel.: 01244 822884 or
01244 815552.
Website: www.dyslexia.uk.com

British Epilepsy Association (also known as Epilepsy Action)

Provides information, advice and support for sufferers and their families.

New Anstey House, Gate Way Drive, Yeadon, Leeds LS19 7NW.

Tel.: 0113 210 8800.

Website: www.epilepsy.org.uk

British Heart Foundation Information

Advice for sufferers, parents and teachers.

14 Fitzhardinge Street, London W1H 6DH.

Tel.: 020 7935 0185.

Website: www.bhf.org.uk

Childline

Free helpline for children needing support with fears regarding bullying, abuse and other problems.

Studd Street, London N1 0QW.

Children's helpline: 0800 1111.

Website: www.childline.org.uk

Clear Vision Project

Materials for visually impaired children. Nationwide postal lending library of children's picture books and Braille and books with tactile features for Key Stages 1 and 2.

Linden Lodge School, 61 Princes Way, London SW19 6JB.

Tel.: 020 8789 9575.

Website: www.clearvisionproject.org

Directory of Key SEN Organizations

Contact-a-Family
Support for families of children with special needs. The CaF Directory has information about a range of conditions. 209–211 City Road, London EC1V 1JN.
Tel.: 020 7608 8700.
Website: www.cafamily.org.uk

Council for Disabled Children
Information about services and facilities for children with disabilities and special needs. National Children's Bureau, 8 Wakley Street, London EC1V 7QE.
Tel.: 020 7843 6061.
Website: www.ncb.org.uk

Deaf Education Through Listening and Talking (DELTA)
Support on hearing impairment in education.
PO Box 20, Haverhill, Suffolk CB9 7BD.
Tel.: 01440 783689.
Website: www.deafeducation.org.uk

Dyscovery Centre
Assessment and advice on dyslexia and dyspraxia.
4a Church Road, Whitchurch, Cardiff CF14 2DZ.
Tel.: 029 2062 8222.
Website: www.dyscovery.co.uk

Dyslexia in Scotland (formerly the Scottish Dyslexia Association)
Advice and support on all aspects of dyslexia.
Stirling Business Centre, Wellgreen, Stirling FK8 2DZ.
Tel.: 01786 446650.
Website: www.dyslexia.scotland.dial.pipex.com

English Sports Association for People with Learning Disability (ESAPLD)

Opportunities for sport for people who have a learning difficulty.
Unit 9, Milner Way, Ossett, West Yorkshire WF5 9JN.
Tel.: 01924 267555.
Website: www.esapld.co.uk

Friends for the Young Deaf (FYD)

Information and support for hearing-impaired children.
120 Abbey Street, Nuneaton CV10 5BY.
Tel.: 024 7635 3766.
Website: www.ndcs.org.uk/fyd/

Hearing Research Trust

Information on all aspects of hearing impairment.
330–332 Gray's Inn Road, London WC1X 8EE.
Tel.: 0808 808 2222.
Website: www.defeatingdeafness.org

Helen Arkell Dyslexia Centre

Support, information, publications and training.
Frensham, Farnham, Surrey GU10 3BW.
Tel.: 01252 792400.
Website: www.arkellcentre.org.uk

IPSEA (The Independent Panel for Special Educational Advice)

Advice to parents from independent experts on all aspects of SEN provision.
6 Carlow Mews, Woodbridge, Suffolk IP12 1DH.
Advice: 0800 018 4016; Scotland: 0131 454 0082;

Northern Ireland: 01232 705654; website:
www.ipsea.org.uk

Kidscape
Information and advice for children. Telephone counselling
for parents.
2 Grosvenor Gardens, London SW61W 0DH.
Tel.: 020 7730 3300.
Website: www.kidscape.org.uk

Kids Link
Provides information and support for parents of children
with SEN.
Website: http://sargon.mmu.ac.uk

National Association for Special Educational Needs (NASEN)
Aims to promote the education, training, advancement and
development of those working with children with SEN.
NASEN House, 4/5 Amber Business Village, Amber Close,
Amington, Tamworth B77 4RP.
Tel.: 01827 311500.
Website: www.nasen.org.uk

National Children's Bureau
Promotes the interests and well-being of all children and
young people.
8 Wakley Street, London EC1B 7QE.
Tel.: 020 7843 6000.
Website: www.ncb.org.uk/about.htm

National Deaf Children's Society (NDCS)

Supports and advises hearing-impaired children and their families.
15 Dufferin Street, London EC1Y 8UR.
Tel.: 020 7490 8656; Helpline: 0808 800 8880.
Website: www.ndcs.org.uk

National Federation of the Blind (UK)

Campaigning for the visually impaired.
Sir John Wilson House, 215 Kirkgate, Wakefield WF1 1JG.
Tel.: 01924 291313.
Website: www.nfbuk.org

National Federation of Families with Visually Impaired Children (LOOK)

Information and support.
Queen Alexandra College, 49 Court Oak Road, Harbourne, Birmingham B17 9TG.
Tel.: 0121 428 5038.
Website: www.look-uk.org

National Fragile X Foundation (USA)

Information on Fragile X Syndrome.
PO Box 190488, San Francisco, California 94119 USA.
Tel.: 00 1 800 688 8765.
Website: www.fragilex.org

National Pyramid Trust

Information on moderate learning difficulties.
Allan Watson, 84 Uxbridge Road, London W13 8RA.
Tel.: 020 8579 5108.
Website: www.nptrust.org.uk

National Society for Prevention of Cruelty to Children (NSPCC)

Therapy and counselling for children and their families.
Western House, 42 Curtain Road, London, EC2A 3NH.
Helpline: 0808 800 5000.
Website: www.nspcc.org.uk

Office for Advice, Assistance, Support and Information on Special Needs (OAASIS)

Information service about various learning disabilities.
Brock House, Grigg Lane, Brockenhurst, Hampshire SO42 7RE.
Helpline: 09068 633201.
Website: www.oaasis.co.uk

Online Asperger Syndrome Information and Support

An award-winning American website for professionals.
Website: www.udel.edu/bkirby/aspeger

Parents for Early Intervention in Autism in Children (PEACH)

Provides information for parents of children with autism.
The Brackens, London Road, Ascot, Berkshire SL5 8BE.
Tel.: 01344 882248.
Website: www.peach.org.uk

Physically Handicapped and Able Bodied (PHAB)

Clubs, activities, outings and holidays.
Summit House, 50 Wandle Road, Croydon CR0 1DF.
Tel.: 020 8667 9443.
Website: www.phabengland.org.uk

RNID (formerly the Royal National Institute for Deaf People)

Publications and educational advice regarding hearing impairment.

19–23 Featherstone Street, London EC1Y 8SL.

Helpline: 0808 808 0123 (Monday–Friday 9am–5pm).

Website: www.rnid.org.uk

Royal National Institute for the Blind (RNIB)

Information, publications and educational advice regarding visual impairment.

105 Judd Street, London WC1H 9NE.

Helpline: 0845 766 9999 (Monday–Friday 9am–5pm).

Website: www.rnib.org.uk

Scottish Society for Autism

Information about autism.

Hilton House, Alloa Business Park, Whins Road, Alloa FK10 3SA.

Tel.: 01259 720044.

Website: www.autism-in-scotland.org.uk

Sense (The National Deaf/Blind and Rubella Association)

Educational advice for parents of children with visual and hearing impairment.

11–13 Clifton Terrace, Finsbury Park, London N4 3SR.

Tel.: 020 7272 7774.

Website: www.sense.org.uk

Special Educational Needs Joint Initiative for Training (SENJIT)

Offers training, support and advice for staff involved in special needs.

Institute of Education, University of London, 20 Bedford Way, London WC1H 0AL.

Website: www.ioe.ac.uk/teepnnp/SENJIT_Home.html

Speech and Language

A website run by two schools. Information for parents about speech and language disorders, including elective mutism.

Website: www.speechnlanguage.org.uk

Speech Teach

Resources for parents and professionals supporting children with speech and learning difficulties.

Website: www.speechteach.co.uk

Visual Impairment Centre for Teaching and Research (VICTAR)

Advice, resources and training.

School of Education, University of Birmingham, Edgbaston, Birmingham B15 2TT.

Tel.: 0121 413 6733; website:
www.education.bham.ac.uk/research/victar

Write Away for Friendship and Communication

Organizes pen-friends for children with disabilities or special needs.

1 Thorpe Close, London W10 5XL.

Tel.: 020 8964 4225; website: www.write-away.org

Appendix 1:
Additional SEN Terms

Anaphylaxis

This is an allergic reaction to a specific source and may be related to a specific food such as peanuts or dairy products but also to insect stings and latex. Symptoms may well involve difficulty in breathing, swallowing and swelling of specific parts of the body.

Treatment only after specific training can involve adrenaline injections, but professional medical help should always be sought.

Diabetes

A condition of blood sugar disorder which means that it is either too high (hyperglycaemia) or too low (hypoglycaemia). The two main types are diabetes mellitus (which is most common) and diabetes insipidus (which is quite rare). Treatment is usually administered by injections of insulin and by maintaining a controlled and regular diet. Glucose tablets or sugary food will need to be available for 'hypo' individuals while monitoring or eliminating high sugar content drinks and foods for 'hyper' individuals

Dyscalculia

This is concerned with deficits in the learning of mathematics. This may include difficulties in understanding and recall of the concept of number, number relationships and difficulties in learning and applying comprehension of word problems. Recent estimates that between three to six per cent of the population is affected by dyscalculia. Dyscalculia may be developmental, in which case the student has always experienced difficulties in the subject; or it may be acquired, in that the student's arithmetic ability was formerly at a higher level than present. Developmental dyscalculia is considered to be a disorder of the abilities to deal with numbers and calculating at an early age, and is not accompanied by coexisting disabilities.

Glue Ear

Also known as otitis media, this can affect many primary children and involves inflammation of the middle ear as a result of accumulation of fluid. It can result in pain and hearing impairment and is often the result of colds and flu. As hearing impairment can cause early issues of speech and language development, the situation is often resolved by inserting grommets to allow fluid to drain from the middle ear. Alternatively, antibiotics and possibly decongestant nasal drops can be used. Professional medical help should always be sought.

Pathological Demand Avoidance (PDA)

This is a pervasive developmental disorder, separate from but related to autism, first identified by Professor Elizabeth Newson at the University of Nottingham in 1983. Children with this syndrome resist and avoid all the 'demands' that are made on them during their normal daily life. The disorder appears to be shared equally between girls and boys. A provisional diagnosis may be possible at around the age of 4, but this is not easy. The child will show more social interest, imaginative skills and normal language development than a child with autism.

Rett Syndrome

This is a severe neurological condition which predominantly affects females. At present there is no treatment or cure, but advances in genetic manipulation may eventually provide answers. Rett Syndrome is a very close second to Down's Syndrome. It is estimated that it occurs in approximately one out of every 10,000 female births (calculated in the USA).

At birth, the baby girls appear normal, and are often unaffected until around the age of one year, when development slows. Further regression develops from around the ages of 1 to 3. It may be sudden or gradual, but parents and professionals will notice loss or withdrawal of skills which had been developing normally, such as social skills, speech, and motor coordination.

Appendix 2:
ADHD Criteria for ADHD
from the DSM IV (1994)

(with permission from the *Diagnostic and Statistical Manual of Mental Disorders*, 1994)

Either (1) or (2):

A. (1) Six (or more) of the following symptoms of inattention have persisted for at least six months to a degree that is maladaptive and inconsistent with developmental level.

Inattention
a) Often fails to give close attention to details or makes careless mistakes in schoolwork or other activities.
b) Often has difficulty in sustaining attention in tasks or play activities.
c) Often does not seem to listen when spoken to directly.
d) Often does not follow through on instructions and fails to finish schoolwork, chores or duties in the workplace (not due to oppositional behaviour or failure to understand instructions).
e) Often has difficulty organizing tasks and activities.
f) Often loses things necessary for tasks and activities (e.g. toys, school assignments, pencils, books or tools).
g) Often avoids, dislikes or is reluctant to engage in tasks that require sustained mental effort (such as school work or homework).
h) Is often easily distracted by extraneous stimuli.
i) Is often forgetful in daily activities.

(2) Six (or more) of the following symptoms of hyperactivity–impulsivity have persisted for at least six months to a degree that is maladaptive/inconsistent with developmental level.

Hyperactivity
a) Often fidgets with hands or feet or squirms in seat.
b) Often leaves seat in classroom or in other situations in which remaining seated is expected.
c) Often runs about or climbs excessively in situations in which it is inappropriate. (In adolescent or adulthood may be limited to subjective feelings of restlessness.)
d) Often has difficulty in playing or engaging in leisure activities quietly.
e) Is often 'on the go' or often acts as if 'driven by a motor'.
f) Often talks excessively.

Impulsiveness
g) Often blurts out answers before questions have been completed.
h) Often has difficulty waiting turn.
i) Often interrupts or intrudes on others (e.g. butts into conversations or games).

B. Some hyperactive–impulsiveness or inattentive symptoms that caused impairment were present before the age of 7 years.

C. Some impairment is present in two or more settings

D. There must be clinically significant impairment in social, academic or occupational functioning.

E. The symptoms do not occur during the course of PDD, schizophrenia or other psychotic disorder and are not better accounted for by another mental disorder.

Appendix 3: Diagnostic Criteria for Conduct Disorder

(with permission from the DSM IV (1994))

A. A repetitive and persistent pattern of behaviour in which the basic rights of others or major age-appropriate societal norms or rules are violated, as manifested by the presence of three (or more) of the following criteria in the past 12 months, with at least one criterion present in the last six months:

Aggression to people and animals
1. Often bullies, threatens or intimidates others.
2. Often initiates physical fights.
3. Has used a weapon that can cause serious physical harm to others (e.g., a bat, brick, broken bottle, knife, gun).
4. Has been physically cruel to people.
5. Has been physically cruel to animals.
6. Has stolen while confronting a victim (e.g. mugging, purse snatching, extortion, armed robbery).
7. Has forced someone into sexual activity.

Destruction of Property
8. Has deliberately engaged in fire setting with the intention of causing serious damage.
9. Has deliberately destroyed others' property (other than by fire setting).

Deceitfulness or theft
10. Has broken into someone else's house, building or car.
11. Often lies to obtain goods or favours or to avoid obligations (i.e. cons others).

12. Has stolen items of non-trivial value without confronting a victim (e.g. shoplifting, but without breaking and entering, forgery).

Serious violations of rules
13. Often stays out at night despite parental prohibitions, beginning before the age of 13 years.
14. Has run away from home overnight at least twice while living in parental or parental surrogate home (or once without returning for a lengthy period).
15. Is often truant from school, beginning before the age of 13 years.

B. The disturbance in behaviour causes clinically significant impairment at social, academic or occupational functioning.

C. If the individual is age 18 years or over, criteria are not met for Antisocial Personality Disorder.

Specify type based on age at onset:

Childhood-Onset Type: Onset of at least one criterion characteristic of Conduct Disorder prior to 10 years of age.
Adolescent-Onset Type: Absence of any criterion characteristic of Conduct Disorder prior to age of 10 years.

Specify severity:

Mild: Few if any conduct problems in excess of those required to make the diagnosis and conduct problems cause only minor harm to others
Moderate: Number of conduct problems and effect on others intermediate between 'mild' and 'severe'.
Severe: Many conduct problems in excess of those required to make the diagnosis or conduct problems cause considerable harm to others.

Appendix 4:
Diagnostic Criteria for
Oppositional Defiant Disorder

(with permission from the DSM IV (1994))

A. A pattern of negativistic, hostile and defiant behaviour lasting at least six months, during which four or more of the following are present:

1. Often loses temper.
2. Often argues with adults.
3. Often actively defies or refuses to comply with adults' requests or rules.
4. Often deliberately annoys people.
5. Often blames others for his or her mistakes or behaviour.
6. Is often touchy or easily annoyed by others.
7. Is often angry or resentful.
8. Is often spiteful and vindictive.

Note: Consider a criterion met only if the behaviour occurs more frequently than is typically observed in individuals of comparable age and developmental level.

B. The disturbance in behaviour causes clinically significant impairment in social, academic or occupational functioning.

C. The behaviours do not occur exclusively during the course of a Psychotic or Mood Disorder.

D. Criteria are not met for Conduct Disorder, and if the individual is aged 18 years or older, criteria are not met for Antisocial Personality Disorder.

Appendix 5:
Characteristics of
Able, Gifted and Talented Children

Not all of the following characteristics will apply to every child, and it is important to emphasize that these children are very often not the obvious 'high achievers' in the classroom.

Verbal abilities
+ Early interest in words, may have read early.
+ May not enjoy the physical act of writing; it slows up the thought processes.
+ Extensive spoken vocabulary, good sentence structure.

Learning styles
+ Learns easily and without apparent effort, masters new concepts without the need for practice.
+ Shows high level of curiosity about the world and how it works; asks penetrating questions.
+ Is keenly observant.
+ Sceptical and persistent when dissatisfied with answers to questions.
+ Recognizes inconsistencies.

Thinking styles
+ Shows great intellectual curiosity: asks deep questions of a philosophical or religious nature.
+ Shows unusual insights.
+ Is able to generalize in an abstract way and extend the scope of discussion from specifics; sees unusual relationships.

- Has wild, sometimes silly ideas; good at guessing.
- Finds unusual solutions to problems.
- Manipulates information.
- Enjoys freewheeling, brainstorming, creating new ideas.

Other areas

- Can have a good understanding of complex mechanical/electrical equipment.
- Can show high levels of accomplishment or potential – often with imagination and creativity – in art, music, drama, sport, etc.

Additional traits

- Can show signs of immaturity – for example temper tantrums, sulking, etc.
- Is inattentive, day-dreams, is lazy; does not complete tasks, makes careless errors.
- Apparent disparity between level of attainment in and out of school.
- Tendency to ask provocative questions.
- Orally very bright; insistent talker but does not write much.
- Some difficulty in learning basic skills, e.g. writing, spelling.
- High level of activity, but undirected.
- Often has difficulty in relationships with children in own age group.

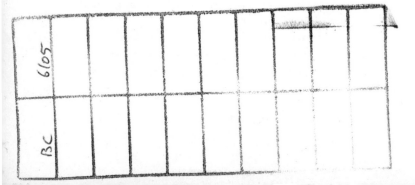